Oral Tradition and the New Testament

GUIDES FOR THE PERPLEXED

Guides for the Perplexed are clear, concise and accessible introductions to thinkers, writers and subjects that students and readers can find especially challenging. Concentrating specifically on what it is that makes the subject difficult to grasp, these books explain and explore key themes and ideas, guiding the reader towards a thorough understanding of demanding material.

Oral Tradition and the New Testament

RAFAEL RODRÍGUEZ

B L O O M S B U R Y

LONDON · NEW DELHI · NEW YORK · SYDNEY

Bloomsbury T&T Clark

An imprint of Bloomsbury Publishing Plc

50 Bedford Square   1385 Broadway
London   New York
WC1B 3DP   NY 10018
UK   USA

www.bloomsbury.com

Bloomsbury is a registered trade mark of Bloomsbury Publishing Plc

First published 2014

© Rafael Rodríguez, 2014

British Library Cataloguing-in-Publication Data
A catalogue record for this book is available from the British Library.

ISBN: HB: 978-0-56760-935-9
PB: 978-0-56762-600-4
ePDF: 978-0-56749-993-6
ePub: 978-0-56744-254-3

Library of Congress Cataloging-in-Publication Data
Rodríguez, Rafael
Oral Tradition and the New Testament / Rafael Rodríguez p.cm
Includes bibliographic references and index.
ISBN 978-0-567-60935-9 (hardcover) – ISBN 978-0-567-62600-4 (pbk.)

Design by Newgen Knowledge Works (P) Ltd., Chennai, India
Printed and bound in India

CONTENTS

LIST OF TABLES

PREFACE

A few hours ago my oldest daughter and I returned home from Disney's *Phineas and Ferb: The Best Live Tour Ever!* At one point toward the end of the show, as Perry the Platypus and the evil Dr. Doofenshmirtz were engaged in their standard climactic battle, something interesting happened. Perry and Dr. Doofenshmirtz were doing their choreographed, pseudo-karate moves as the lights flashed around them. Suddenly, somehow, both of them had lighted swords that, in another context, would have looked like lightsabers, and the combatants switched from staged punches and kicks to staged thrusts and parries. At the same time, the typical Phineas-and-Ferb style alternative rock music faded just a bit, and over the top of the heavily distorted guitars came the sounds of John Williams' *Star Wars* music. In the end, of course, Perry was victorious and Dr. Doofenshmirtz was vanquished.

The sights and sounds of the show caught my interest for a couple of reasons that are relevant for this book. First, the multisensory allusion to the *Star Wars* epic gave added depth to what everyone in the audience already knew: the battle between Perry and Doofenshmirtz was a battle between good and evil. Second, for the parents in the audience who grew up in the shadow of the war between the Rebel Alliance and the Galactic Empire, the allusion enabled us to join our children and experience (at least part of) the show from the vantage of our childhood. Third, the duel between Perry and Doofenshmirtz did not call to my mind a particular scene from any of the six *Star Wars* movies; it summoned the entire *Star Wars* epic all at once (and, I should add, in just a couple of seconds). Fourth, judging from the reaction of the kids in the audience, anyone who did not pick up the allusion (my daughter did not) nevertheless continued to enjoy the show despite not having access to this added depth. And finally, fifth, watching Perry and Doofenshmirtz parry and thrust their lightsabers raised some fairly odd questions, especially: Is Dr. Doofenshmirtz Perry the Platypus's father? All of this from two lighted swords and a couple of measures of familiar music!

The writers and choreographers of *Phineas and Ferb: The Best Live Tour Ever!* managed to creatively interweave their narrative of a crime-fighting platypus into the larger cultural tradition of good and evil embodied in the *Star Wars* space epic. No one needed them to explain why they included the allusion, nor did anyone need them to explain what it meant. It just "worked," because the writers creatively included traditional material into their musical score and their choreography and because the audience was prepared to interpret their intention.

This book argues that something similar happened for the earliest Christians when they gathered to tell stories from and about Jesus, to hear the old sacred traditions about Moses, David, and the prophets recounted, or to witness a public performance of a letter from Paul or James or Peter. When Mark tells us that the Spirit of God "cast out" (*ekballō*) Jesus into the wilderness to be tested by the satan, that unusual word—*ekballō*—opened a window onto a much larger traditional world. Like a lightsaber in the hands of a giant green platypus, the connection with a larger, encompassing tradition added a layer of meaning to the narrative.[1] The allusion is subtle, and certainly some of Mark's readers would have missed it. But that hardly matters. The allusion is there, for those with "ears to hear."

The twentieth century saw a massive rise of interest in oral tradition and the New Testament. Early in the century, the form critics—especially Martin Dibelius and Rudolf Bultmann—were largely responsible for raising the issue, but by the end of the century most students of the NT were dissatisfied with how they handled the dynamics and consequences of oral tradition. In the second half of the century, interdisciplinary research from Homeric studies, cultural anthropology, and other fields offered alternative ways to address questions of oral tradition. In the 1980s and 1990s, NT scholars began to take increasingly sophisticated account of these alternative ways, especially in the wake of Werner Kelber's seminal book, *The Oral and the Written Gospel* (1983). The explosion of media-critical work has not only continued but accelerated in the first decade-plus of the twenty-first century. Even so, the media-critical analysis of NT texts is comparatively young, still merely a babe in the shadow of its elder siblings: historical criticism, literary criticism, and the rest of the family.

This book sets out to introduce the basic elements of NT media criticism, which I define as "the analysis of the function and dynamics of various media of communication (speech, writing, ritual, etc.), and especially of the significance of shifts from one medium to another (e.g., from oral to written expression)." I have tried to provide broad discussions of the field. Even so, at every step I provide analytical and evaluative discussions rather than disinterested, objective summaries of the current state of NT media criticism. In other words, this book is more than an introduction to NT media criticism. It is also my proposal for the future agenda of NT media criticism.

A number of people have been helpful at various stages of the production of this book. Dominic Mattos was receptive to the idea of a volume on oral tradition in the Guides for the Perplexed series when I pitched it to him in Atlanta at an SBL Annual Meeting. Timothy Gombis and James Crossley, both of whom contributed their own Guides for the Perplexed (Gombis 2010; Crossley 2010), helped me think about what an introduction to oral tradition and the NT should look like. Chris Keith provided invaluable feedback and encouragement for this project. The editorial staff at T&T Clark International, especially Caitlin Flynn, has been remarkably flexible when I had to push back a deadline once or twice (or thrice!). I would like to thank Chris Davis and the administration of Johnson University for my Sabbatical during the Fall 2012 term; the majority of this volume was written during that time. The library staff at Johnson University, especially Jon Hale and Heidi Berryhill, have answered my every request for any article or book, and they have always done so cheerily. Lydia Wade worked through nearly the entire manuscript and provided invaluable editorial assistance. I should also mention that, late in the production of this volume, I learned of Eric Eve's forthcoming volume, *Behind the Gospels: Understanding the Oral Tradition* (SPCK). Unfortunately, I was not able to take account of Eric's work, but he graciously supplied me with a pre-publication copy of his manuscript.

Of course, the lion's share of my appreciation goes to my wife, Andrea, and our daughters, Janelle and Josephina. They have often permitted me to linger at my computer when there were chores to be done, games to be played, homework to be completed, stories to be read, and so on. More importantly (and more often), they have *not* let me linger at my computer when the chores, games, homework, and stories beckoned. Their persistence makes me the husband and father I am, and if the quality of this book suffers just a little bit (and hopefully *no more than* just a little bit), I am fine with that.

On Saturday, September 22, 2012, my sister Rikki Erin Bera (née Sommervold) finished her fight with cancer. She was 29 years old, which is much too young. I dedicate this book to her memory.

Rafael Rodríguez
Johnson University
February 15, 2013

CHAPTER ONE

Introduction

In the spring of 2004 I began reading scholarship on oral tradition and oral historiography (i.e. history-writing that depends on information gathered in interviews with witnesses to and/or participants in past events).[1] For six months I read about Basque-separatist women's memories of struggles against the Spanish government, contemporary African techniques for preserving and narrating the past, the contribution of oral interviews to our understanding of the internment of Japanese American citizens during WWII, the oral and written techniques of information management and social engagement in ancient Greece, and dozens of other topics that scholars have studied from the perspective of oral tradition and history.

Despite all this exposure to so-called orality studies, I found myself woefully unprepared to understand John Miles Foley's groundbreaking book, *The Singer of Tales in Performance*, when I picked it up in May 2005. The material was complicated and full of concepts and terms I did not know and could not understand. And I had been reading about oral tradition for over a year! But some books are worth the effort it takes to understand them. *The Singer of Tales in Performance* was one of these. When I finally began to understand him, John Miles Foley fundamentally changed the way I think about the early Christians, how they spoke with one another about Jesus, how they understood written accounts of Jesus' life and teachings (what we call "Gospels"), and how we, two millennia later, should understand those Gospels.

But not everyone has the time or the energy (or the interest!) to wade through complex, technical books about oral tradition. Add to this the problem that there simply are not very many tools to help bring the study of oral tradition within the reach of undergraduate and/or graduate and Seminary students. Too often the technical jargon alone makes such scholarship out-of-reach. In this book I hope to help solve these problems. This book has two goals. The chapters in Part One offer explanations of the various terms and concepts that students can expect to encounter as they read oral-traditional research. Then, in Part Two, we will demonstrate how such research opens up fresh understandings of the NT texts. My goal is to unpack the technicalities of how scholars think about oral tradition rather than to avoid those technicalities.

But is not the New Testament a written text?

No. Well . . . yes. The NT contains 27 texts, and all of them were written sometime during the first-century CE. And while none of the original texts, called "autographs," still exist today, we do have literally thousands of handwritten copies. These range from tiny fragments of only a couple of square inches to copies of the entire NT.[2] So no, the NT is not *a* written text; it is a *collection* of texts. And yes, it is a collection of *written* texts.

We might find ourselves asking, "Then what does oral tradition have to do with the NT?" Perhaps the most obvious fact—so obvious we hardly need say it out loud—is that we do not have one single syllable of early Christian oral tradition. Not one sound recording or video of first-century Christians talking about Jesus remains today. All we have are our written texts. Moreover, none of the NT texts appear to be transcriptions or descriptions of an oral performance of the Jesus tradition. We also have a wealth of material artifacts that archaeologists have unearthed: coins, pottery, tools, and so on. These help illumine the world in which the earliest Christians lived. But for the most part, we rely on written texts to know about Jesus and the earliest Christians. There simply is no oral tradition for us to study.[3] Everything we think we know about the first-century CE comes from a text that somebody once wrote and that, through accident, diligent copying and preservation, or both, survived until today. There is no first-century oral Jesus tradition. Period.

Even so, every indication leads us to think that the earliest Christians told the stories about Jesus in a number of different communications media, both oral and written. Consider the following, all of which suggest that oral and written media interacted in important but complex ways:

- **Scholars estimate that literacy rates in the ancient world were shockingly low.** The CIA World Factbook estimates that the United States enjoyed a 99 percent literacy rate in 2003.[4] Reading is such a standard part of life in Western culture that it does not even register in our everyday consciousness. We read street signs, menus, billboards, news tickers, product descriptions, and myriad other written texts so often and effortlessly that reading is like breathing: Everyone is doing it. Things could not have been more different in the Roman world. William Harris (1989) and Catherine Hezser (2001) both estimate that less than 10 percent—and perhaps closer to 3 percent—of the total population in Roman Palestine (urban and rural, male and female, etc.) could read.[5] Chris Keith (2011a) has even raised the question whether Jesus himself could write and/or read.[6] In the ancient world, then, most people did not encounter stories about Jesus in written texts because most people could not read written texts.

- **Inhabitants of Roman Judea and Herodian Galilee lived in the shadow of written texts.** Despite the relative lack of literacy in the ancient world, written texts were everywhere. First, of course, must be the written texts of the Hebrew Bible, which cast their shadow over the entire region.[7] Both Mark and Matthew refer to "the scriptures" (*hai graphai*) only during the Jerusalem phase of Jesus' ministry.[8] John uses the word *graphē* ("scripture") more than the other Evangelists combined, but, like Mark and Matthew, confines his uses of *graphē* to Jerusalem and Judea.[9] Unlike Matthew, Mark, and John, Luke locates biblical texts in Galilee (Lk. 4.16–21) and refers to their distribution outward from Jerusalem (Acts 8.27–35). We should also mention the large number of texts found in the Judean desert, from biblical, sectarian, and liturgical texts among the famous Dead Sea Scrolls to the Bar Kokhba letters and Babatha cache found at Naḥal Ḥever. Despite the fact that relatively few people could actually read from written scrolls, Jewish culture in the first centuries BCE and CE demonstrated "an appreciation for texts among the general population" (Hurtado 1997:96).[10]

● **Even in the shadow of written texts, the earliest Christians continued to place a high value on orally expressed tradition.** Papias, a bishop in Hieropolis (western Asia Minor [modern-day Turkey]), provides an important example of this high value. I quote him at length:

> I will not hesitate to set down for you, along with my interpretations, everything I carefully learned then from the elders and carefully remembered, guaranteeing their truth. For unlike most people I did not enjoy those who have a great deal to say, but those who teach the truth. Nor did I enjoy those who recall foreign commandments, but those who remember the commandments given by the Lord to the faith and proceeding from the truth itself. And if by chance someone who had been a follower of the elders should come my way, I inquired about the words of the elders—what Andrew or Peter said, or Philip or Thomas or James or John or Matthew or any other of the Lord's disciples, and whatever Aristion and the elder John, the Lord's disciples, were saying. *For I did not think that things found in books would benefit me as much as things from a living and abiding voice.* (Papias, frag. 3.3–4 [Holmes; modified]; emphasis added).[11]

Scholars have spilled considerable ink over this passage.[12] South African NT scholar, Pieter Botha, rightly concludes that Christians in the first centuries CE were not predestined to produce written texts, but he goes on to imply that some Christians, such as Papias, would not have even wanted to produce written texts.[13] Others, such as British NT scholar Richard Bauckham, have reacted too sharply in the opposite direction and denied that

Papias prefers authoritative oral tradition over written tradition.[14] I think the proper approach lies between these extremes: Papias clearly sees writing as a useful medium of instruction; after all, he is *writing a five-volume book* on the teachings of Jesus![15] Even so, Papias clearly prefers to learn what he can "straight from the horse's mouth" rather than by reading it from a written source. "[R]egardless of whether Papias preferred oral or written tradition, what he wanted was *tradition*. This tradition was handed down in several ways, and in the handing down was retold and rewritten" (Parker 1997:204). The traditional written word sufficed; the traditional spoken word more than sufficed.

● **The earliest Christians nevertheless exhibited a keen interest in written texts from the very beginning.** Jesus, of course, never wrote anything that lasted.[16] If we judge them by the number of books they wrote, the early Christians were significantly more productive than Jesus. Paul, who apparently did not know Jesus personally, began writing the letters we have in the NT within about 20 years after Jesus' death. The Gospel of Mark, which is the earliest of the four Gospels according to most NT scholars, was likely written just before the war with Rome (66–70 CE), though it might have been written much earlier.[17] By the end of the first-century CE and the beginning of the second, Christians had written numerous texts: letters,[18] handbooks,[19] homilies,[20] historical works of various kinds,[21] and other texts besides.[22] We can therefore agree with Harry Gamble's assessment of the early church: "[F]rom the very beginning Christianity was deeply engaged in the interpretation and appropriation of texts. . . . [E]arly Christianity was never without a literary dimension" (1995:27, 29).

These four points—(1) the low levels of literacy in antiquity, (2) the robust textuality of Hellenistic and Roman Judaism, (3) the preference for direct (oral) authority, and (4) the broad range of early Christian text-production—demonstrate the complexity of the question of communications media (oral, written, and others) among the early Christians.

What do NT scholars mean by "orality"?

A quick search through my university's library reveals titles such as *Orality and Literacy* (Ong 1982), *Orality, Aurality and Biblical Narrative* (Silberman 1987), and *The Interface of Orality and Writing* (Weissenrieder and Coote 2010). Other books, such as Werner Kelber's seminal work, *The Oral and the Written Gospel* (1983), or *Oral Tradition and Literary Dependency* (Mournet 2005), or *Jesus, the Voice, and the Text* (Thatcher 2008), may not use the word "orality" in their titles, but when you start reading through them you encounter the word fairly quickly and very often. An even quicker search through the American Theological Library Association database (ATLA) turns up over 100 articles and essays with orality in their titles. Everyone seems to be talking about "orality."

So we might be somewhat surprised to discover that scholars are not very clear about what "orality" means. Rosalind Thomas, a historian of ancient Greece, points out that "orality" often refers to different things at the same time. Sometimes "orality" means "communication without written texts," but at other times it refers to certain qualities of written texts (Thomas 1992:6–8). Ruth Finnegan (1990) complains that when scholars refer to "orality," they act as if the word refers to something specific and universal, like how the word "water" refers to the same thing in every culture. Unfortunately, "orality" is not like "water." Orality refers to any number of things, from oral communication in pre- and/or nonliterate societies to oral communication in societies with varying access to writing. Sometimes orality refers to the oral expression and interpretation of *written* texts. Orality can even refer to wider social and/or cultural characteristics, including "a lack of concern for original forms and authorship, extreme respect for rhetorical skill, placing greater value on interpersonal interaction than on abstract sets of values and logical deductions, and stress on the community rather than on individualism and individual thought" (Davis 2008:754).

In light of these broader uses of orality, we can begin to understand how some scholars can refer to "the oral characteristics" of written texts (e.g. of the Gospel of Mark; see Dewey 1989). William Graham even uses the oxymoronic phrase "oral text" to refer to a written text that demonstrates an "oral/aural character," a "functional orality" by virtue of being read and recited orally (1987:36).[23] Understandably, given all the various things "orality" can mean (including certain qualities of written texts!), John Miles Foley, a leading writer on oral and written tradition, complained, "Orality alone is a 'distinction' badly in need of deconstruction . . . it is by itself a false and misleading category" (1995a:170). Media critics use the word "orality" to avoid the word "illiteracy," which refers to the inability to read and/or write. Unlike "illiteracy," "orality" does not refer to an *in*ability; it refers to a different set of abilities than does the word "literacy." Unfortunately, it does not get any more specific than that.

I will therefore avoid referring to orality throughout this volume, except when citing scholars who do use the term. In Chapter Four, I will discuss in detail what I think is the most unfortunate result of all our talk of orality and our failure to be clear and precise about what orality is. That is, we have continued to ask the same question biblical scholars have been asking since at least the nineteenth century: How were the NT texts written?[24] In the study of the Gospels, this question has been called "source criticism," which Mark Strauss has defined as a "type of historical criticism which seeks to identify the written sources behind each Gospel and their relationship to one another" (2007:538). In their very popular introduction to the NT, Carson et al. introduce source criticism with explicit recognition of an "oral stage" of the Jesus tradition:

> The oral stage of the development of the Synoptic Gospels . . . probably also included some written traditions about Jesus' life and teachings. Some of the apostles may have taken notes on Jesus' teachings and activities during the ministry itself, and they and other eyewitnesses probably accelerated that process after the resurrection. But it is probable that a predominantly oral period of transmission only eventually gave way to a period during which more substantial bodies of written tradition began to be produced, in a procedure that led eventually to the canonical Gospels. Source criticism is devoted to the investigation of this written stage in the production of the Gospels. It asks, and seeks to answer, this question: What written sources, if any, did the evangelists use in compiling their gospels? (1992:26)[25]

A number of orality studies, as we will see more fully in Chapter Four, continue this emphasis on the production and/or composition of the NT texts. As a result they conceive of "orality" as a source that contributed to the final form of the texts we now have. Instead of focusing on the *composition* of NT texts, we will turn our attention toward questions of the tradition's development, expression, and transmission. We will also address the early Christians' production, reception, and transmission of written texts. "Orality," however, will have very little to contribute to this discussion. Rather than attempting to tease apart the compositional dynamics of early Christian written texts (and the role of oral sources in their composition), we will consistently and intentionally address issues of the interplay between multiple communicative media, especially the oral expression of tradition.

Are we still studying the written texts of the NT, or something else?

We have already acknowledged that no early Christian oral tradition survives today. All that we have are the written texts of the period and material remains unearthed by archaeologists. The title of this book reflects this basic fact. I called this book *Oral Tradition and the New Testament* because I want to explore how the interdisciplinary study of oral tradition can help us study the written texts of the NT. But we should never lose sight of the fact that we are, at the end of the day and all day long, studying written texts.

New Testament scholars have a history of forgetting this very thing. Rudolf Bultmann and Martin Dibelius, two giants of German NT form criticism, were explicit about their intention to move beyond (or behind) the written texts of the Gospels and recover the prewritten oral Jesus tradition. For example, according to Dibelius form criticism (= *Formgeschichte*) has two goals: "In the first place, by reconstruction and analysis, it seeks to explain the origin of the tradition about Jesus, and thus *to penetrate into a period previous to that in which our Gospels and their written sources were recorded*. But it has a further purpose. It seeks to make clear the intention and real interest of the earliest tradition"

(1935:v; my emphasis). Similarly, Bultmann's scholarship began from "the fundamental assumption that the tradition consists of individual stories or groups of stories joined together in the Gospels by the work of the editors" (1963:2). The form critics thought they could recover these "individual stories or groups of stories" by dissolving the Gospels' narrative frameworks and analyzing each story individually.[26] So when they isolated, for example, the story of Jesus walking on the water (Mk 6.45–52 parr.) from its narrative context, they proceeded as if they had penetrated through the written Gospels and discovered the pre-Gospel tradition—whether oral or written—of the earliest Christian communities (see Bultmann 1963:216; 226–31; Dibelius 1935:116).

New Testament scholars have long-since abandoned the naïve assumption that we could actually recover the pre-Gospel oral Jesus tradition simply by undoing the Gospels' narrative frameworks—their plot structures, their transitional material, and so on—and analyzing each pericope outside its current literary context. Nevertheless, even today we run the risk of thinking that all of this talk of "oral tradition" refers to anything other than the written texts we have before us. Even the father of contemporary NT media criticism, Werner Kelber, imagines he has recovered the prewritten, pre-Markan "unorganized oral lore" that existed before the written text of Mark's Gospel that we have today (1983:77–80; 79 cited). We simply do not know anything concrete or specific about early Christian oral tradition. Consider the following, very basic, questions, none of which have any conclusive answers:

- How often did Christian communities gather for oral performances of the Jesus tradition?
- How long were such performances?
- What functions did such performances play within the community?
- Who was permitted (or expected) to recount the tradition?
- What role, if any, did written texts play in such performances?

And we could go on. The only things we have for sure are our written texts. We can make inferences beyond our written texts, but those inferences will always remain inferential. For all the talk of oral tradition among NT scholars, we must remember that we are only ever studying and explaining *written*—not *oral*—tradition.

In the following chapters (esp. Chapters Four and Five), we will use the term "oral-derived text" to highlight questions of oral tradition and to remind ourselves at every step that we are engaging written texts. The term "oral-derived text" comes from John Miles Foley's technical but groundbreaking work, especially *Immanent Art* (1991) and *The Singer of Tales in Performance* (1995a). Foley uses this term to refer to "works of verbal art that either stem directly from or have roots in oral tradition" (1991:xi; see Rodríguez 2010:35–7). His work addresses both entirely textual remains of once-vibrant oral tradition (Homer's *Iliad*, or the Old English epic *Beowulf*) as well as genuine and actual *oral* tradition (the Moslem songs from the Serbo-Croatian tradition). But even in his analyses of actual oral traditions, Foley has to navigate and account for the problem of how to represent all the features of an oral performance in written text. When the meaning of the words of an oral text depend on nonverbal things such as tone, gesture, pace, or body language, how do we transcribe the oral text into written text? Or, when we only have the written textual remnants of a once-oral tradition, how do we account for the influence of nonverbal communication on the meaning of our texts? Questions such as these push Foley to attempt "whenever possible to supplement an analysis that must (even by default) be based primarily on texts with a sense of the larger traditional context from which all of these events-become-texts must take their meaning" (Foley 1991:xi, n. 2). Note Foley's phrase, "these events-become-texts." We are always trying to infer something about the oral-performative *events* implied by our written texts. In the field of NT scholarship, we are always ultimately bound to the interpretation of written *texts*.

What is the plan of this book?

The bulk of this book occurs in the following four chapters. Part One will *introduce the field of biblical media criticism*. First, because much of the discussion is so technical and abstract, Chapter Two will define some of the technical jargon that students can expect to encounter when they pick up the burgeoning scholarship of oral tradition and the NT. This chapter provides a glossary of technical terms, including simple, rough-but-serviceable definitions of some of the most common terms readers can expect to encounter. Chapter Three will then provide a brief account of the rise of awareness of and interest in questions of oral tradition in the aftermath of the twentieth-century form critics. Beginning with Birger Gerhardsson, whose lone prophetic voice challenged the form critics at the height of their influence, we will mention some of the key figures in the discussion of oral tradition and the NT and their seminal contributions.

Part Two will *demonstrate the field of biblical media criticism.* Chapter Four highlights two approaches to NT media criticism. As we have already mentioned, one approach emphasizes issues of composition and sources (and so focuses on morphological features of the text, as we will explain in Chapter Four). A second approach, which I prefer, highlights the analysis of written texts— their composition as well as their expression, reception, and transmission—within the context of a vibrant oral tradition. Chapter Five, then, provides four short, topical examples that illustrate how oral-traditional research can contribute to the interpretation of our written texts. This chapter emphasizes exegesis as the goal of biblical scholarship. Questions of oral tradition have to make an impact at the exegetical level in order to justify the attention they have been receiving in recent scholarship. These short examples demonstrate that, in fact, the effort it takes to become proficient in working with oral-traditional research does indeed supply an exegetical payoff.

PART ONE

An introduction to biblical media criticism

CHAPTER TWO

The *what* of oral tradition and NT studies

Media criticism involves a number of unfamiliar words and complicated concepts, both of which can make readers entering the arena of media criticism for the first time feel like they are deciphering the painted walls of Egypt's Valley of the Kings. Consider the following, which I have taken almost at random:

> The stories we have studied exhibit full narrative self-sufficiency. This repays our attention because recent literary criticism has habituated us to seeing the small units as integral parts of the compositional whole. Eminently important as the literary comprehension of the gospel narratives is, we must not lose sight of the fact that many of their component parts represent modes of oral integrity. Our use of them in worship and instruction amply demonstrates their ability to function as self-contained oral units of communication. (Kelber 1983:79)

Students would be forgiven for wondering if Kelber is making a point about the Gospel of Mark or explaining how to clean a carburettor. In fact, Kelber is getting to the heart of his approach to accounting for "oral hermeneutics" and the written Gospel of Mark, so this is a vitally important text. But Kelber is not writing for students, so his point may lie at the edges of, if not quite beyond, their comprehension.

But it need not be so. The purpose of this volume is not to avoid complicated discussions but rather to bring them closer to the ground so that they are more broadly accessible. Our present task, then, is to lay a foundation for the media-critical discussions in Part Two. This chapter provides a glossary of some of the more common technical terminology readers will encounter in media-critical NT scholarship. In some ways the decisions about which words to include and which to exclude are arbitrary, but hopefully this list will make most media-critical concepts and analyses accessible. I have tried to provide broadly acceptable definitions to these terms, though specialists may find reason to argue with some, qualify others, or extend and expand yet others. Nevertheless, the present chapter sets out to provide rough but accurate and helpful definitions of key terms and concepts.

Some of the terms in this list are new and unfamiliar to most readers (e.g. chirograph or psychodynamics). Other terms are already familiar to most readers, but media critics use them differently, or with special meanings. As a result, I have included some already familiar words (e.g. audience or literacy) in order to explain some of the nuance these words may convey in media-critical scholarship.

Some readers might find it helpful to read through this chapter before moving on to the chapters in Part Two. Others might prefer to get stuck right into the more technical discussions to follow and refer back to this chapter when they encounter unfamiliar terms or concepts. The format of this book hopefully accommodates both kinds of readers.

Glossary of terms

AUDIENCE
A broad term referring to the receivers of a communication, whether oral, written, monumental, and so on. Media critics emphasize the audience's role in creating and interpreting the text of an oral performance or of an oral-derived text. Exactly how an audience contributes to the text of a performance varies in different media, but in every medium they influence the final form of the communication. For example, in an oral performance the

performer may react to feedback from the audience as she tells a story, whether to explain a misunderstood point or to emphasize a theme that resonates with the audience. In a public reading of a written manuscript (whose wording is comparatively fixed), an audience may affect the lector's pace, tone, gestures, and other prosodic dynamics of the performative event.

AURALITY

Having to do with the ear and/or with hearing, and especially with those features of written texts that appear designed especially to register with listening audiences.

BIOSPHERE

1 A metaphor introduced by Werner Kelber in 1995 to refer to the relationship between an abstract tradition and a specific oral performance or oral-derived text that expresses that tradition. "Tradition in this encompassing sense is a circumambient contextuality or biosphere in which speaker and hearers live. It includes texts and experiences transmitted through or derived from texts. But it is anything but reducible to intertextuality. Tradition in this broadest sense is largely an invisible nexus of references and identities from which people draw sustenance, in which they live, and in relation to which they make sense of their lives. This invisible biosphere is at once the must elusive and the foundational feature of tradition" (Kelber 1995:159; see also Foley 1995b:171). As a metaphor, the term "biosphere" highlights how previous performances of a tradition provide an invisible but ever-present context within which audiences receive and interpret later oral performances and/or written versions of that tradition. *See* circumambient; economy, communicative; immanence; Immanent Art; metonymy.

2 Tom Thatcher uses Kelber's metaphor as a synonym for Kelber's idea of an "oral synthesis" (see Thatcher 2008:4). Kelber, however, does not use "biosphere" in quite this way. *See* oral synthesis.

CHIROGRAPH

A manuscript (Greek *cheir* ["hand"; = Lat. *manus*] + *graphē* ["writing"; = Lat. *scriptus*]). Media critics use the less-familiar term to highlight differences between a handwritten (chiro + graph) manuscript and other media, especially oral speech, on the one hand, and printed texts, on the other.

CIRCUMAMBIENT
All-encompassing and ever-present. This term usually describes the presence of tradition as a larger context that gives meaning to a written text, oral performance, or other individual expression of tradition. *See* biosphere.

COMPOSITION-IN-PERFORMANCE
The extemporaneous composition of an oral text during an oral performance. The text that is composed-in-performance is neither original nor innovative; it is traditional. However, the text is also not an exact copy of any previous oral text; it is an autonomous and authentic text on its own. Albert Lord described the phenomenon as follows: "The singer's mode of composition is dictated by the demands of performance at high speed, and he depends upon inculcated habit and association of sounds, words, phrases, and lines. He does not shrink from the habitual; nor does he either require the fixed for memorization or seek the unusual for its own sake. His oft-used phrases and lines lose something in sharpness, yet many of them must resound with overtones from the dim past whence they came" (1960:65). *See* economy; formula; Oral-Formulaic Theory.

ECONOMY
The concept developed by Milman Parry and Albert Lord, which they also called "thrift," to explain how oral performers could compose-in-performance complex and lengthy epic tales (in excess of 10,000 lines) within a structured musical and metrical system. Economy refers to "the degree in which [a formula type or system] is free of phrases which, having the same metrical value and expressing the same idea, could replace one another" (Foley 1988:24–5). In other words, the principle of "economy" means that oral poets did not generally have multiple ways to communicate the same idea in the same conditions, so they did not get bogged down choosing among equally viable synonyms. *See* composition-in-performance; formula; Oral-Formulaic Theory.

ECONOMY, COMMUNICATIVE
The ability of a word or phrase to communicate extra information (= connotative value) in traditional contexts, for example, in an oral traditional performance or an oral-derived text. Under the right social, rhetorical, and performative conditions, words

or phrases can function "as an index-point or node in a grand, untextualizable network of traditional associations. Activation of any single node brings into play an enormous wellspring of meaning that can be tapped in no other way, no matter how talented or assiduous the performer may be" (Foley 1995a:54). When used in a traditional register and/or in an appropriate performance arena, words take on additional, extra meaning; this is "communicative economy." Readers should take care not to confuse the principle of "communicative economy," associated with John Miles Foley's development of Immanent Art, with the Parry-Lord principle of "thrift," or "economy." *See* immanence; Immanent Art; metonymy; performance arena; register.

ENTEXTUALIZATION
The process of fixing the wording of a tradition, which usually (perhaps inevitably) results in the text's separation from its "biosphere," the "grand, untextualizable network of traditional associations" (Foley 1995a:54). As it progresses, entextualization results in a fixed text (often referred to as "the original text," which can be oral or written) that is more or less severed from its circumambient tradition. As the words used to express a tradition become increasingly fixed, those words become more concrete in meaning and lose their communicative economy. *See* biosphere; economy, communicative.

EQUIPRIMORDIALITY
The principle that multiple expressions of an utterance are all equally original, that each expression is "an original version, and in fact *the original version*" (Kelber 1995:151; emphasis in the original). Equiprimordiality denies the possibility of seeking a specific and individual "original version" because every expression is original, autonomous, and authentic. *See* multiformity; plurality.

ETHNOPOETICS
An academic discipline that "addresses how to translate and transcribe oral performances while seeking to maintain the artistic value of such verbal art" (Maxey 2009:16). Ethnopoetics attempts to address the problem of transcribing more than the verbal content of an oral tradition, to account for the non- and paralinguistic features that affect the reception, interpretation, transmission, and social significance of an oral tradition (see Bauman 1992a).

EVENT

The social experience by which an audience participates in an oral performance of a tradition or a public reading of an oral-derived text. Media critics, especially under Kelber's influence, emphasize that "oral words, unlike printed words, are events in time rather than objects in space" (Thatcher 2011:39). *See* oral synthesis.

FORMULA

A regularly recurring phrase ("stock phrase") with a fixed metrical value that enables the rapid composition-in-performance of strictly oral epic songs. After the publication of Albert Lord's *The Singer of Tales* (1960), scholars interpreted the presence of formulas in a written text as an indication of oral tradition and composition-in-performance. Such an assumption is now generally discredited, especially in relation to the Jesus tradition and the Gospels (see Rodríguez 2010:23–4). *See* composition-in-performance; economy; Oral-Formulaic Theory.

GREAT DIVIDE, THE

A widely discredited approach to oral and written tradition that assumes that oral and written media are fundamentally different and distinct. Nearly every media critic distances her- or himself from the Great Divide theory of communicative media,[1] but this theory remains influential even in current scholarship (e.g. see Davis 2008; Kelber and Thatcher 2008:29–30; Loubser 2007:10–11).

HOMEOSTASIS

The quality of forgetting or not preserving aspects of the past that are not immediately relevant for current social or cultural needs, particularly in oral cultures. "[W]hatever parts of [the memory of the past] have ceased to be of contemporary relevance are likely to be eliminated by the process of forgetting. . . . What continues to be of social relevance is stored in memory while the rest is usually forgotten" (Goody and Watt 1968:6). Proponents of homeostatic views of oral cultures argue that such cultures have little if any awareness of the past as a period distinct from the present. For example, "[O]ral societies live very much in a present which keeps itself in equilibrium or homeostasis by sloughing off memories which no longer have present relevance" (Ong 1982:46).

IMMANENCE

The always-present, expanded meaning—or "extra information"—
that provides the context within which an oral performer and her/
his audience interpret the words, gestures, and other features of
an oral performance or an oral-derived text. An oral performance
or an oral-derived text must signal its connection to this "extra
information" through preestablished and agreed-upon clues that
communicate the traditional nature of the text's contents. Foley
defines *immanence* as "the set of metonymic, associative meanings
institutionally delivered and received through a dedicated idiom
or register either during or on the authority of traditional oral
performance" (1995a:7). *See* register; economy, communicative.

IMMANENT ART

John Miles Foley's adaptation of the Parry-Lord theory of oral
composition, which moves beyond an analysis of a tradition's
formulaic language to consider how a tradition's formulaic
language generates meaning, especially by linking an oral text or
an oral-derived text to its circumambient (= extratextual) tradition
(see Foley 1991; 1995a:2–7). Immanent Art can be roughly
summarized by Foley's slogan, "Tradition is the enabling referent,
performance the enabling event" (1995a:xiii). *See* biosphere;
economy, communicative; immanence; Oral-Formulaic Theory;
metonymy; traditional referentiality.

LECTOR

A reader, especially in a liturgical or similar ritual context. In light
of the visually demanding aspects of ancient chirographs (which
lacked, for the most part, paragraph divisions, punctuation, and
even spaces between words), media critics often claim that lectors
had to have memorized, more or less, the texts they read. For
this reason, many media critics portray lectors as *performers* of
the tradition more than *readers* in the modern sense. (But see
Johnson 2010:17–22, who points out that the ancient sources do
not complain of the difficulty of reading ancient texts and offers
explanations why.) Pieter Botha provides a helpful description of
what a lector does: "Reading in antiquity was not experienced as
a silent scanning, mainly mental activity. It was a performative,
vocal, oral-aural event. The reader literally recited, with vocal and
bodily gestures, the text which one usually memorised beforehand"
(2005:622).

LITERACY

1 The ability to read written texts.

2 The ability to write written texts.

LITERACY, CRAFTSMAN

"[T]he condition in which the majority, or a near-majority, of skilled craftsmen are literate, while women and unskilled labourers and peasants are mainly not" (Harris 1989:8). Craftsman literates could use and decipher written texts as necessary for the function of their trade, but the more socially significant texts of scripture and literature were beyond their grasp (see also Keith 2011a:112–14). *See* literacy, scribal.

LITERACY, SCRIBAL

The ability to read, interpret, and explain significant written texts, including especially religious (scriptures) and literary texts. Scribal literates enjoy a level of social prestige and power, and they function as authoritative keepers of culture, tradition, and social identity (see Keith 2011a:110–12). Questions of ancient literacy in first-century Jewish culture (including the early Christians) are typically concerned with scribal literacy, especially since historians and exegetes focus on the reading of sacred texts in particular (rather than business receipts, marriage contracts, and so on). *See* literacy, craftsman.

LITERACY, TRADESMAN

See literacy, craftsman.

MANUSCRIPT

A text written by hand, usually on papyrus or parchment. The use of the word "manuscript" as a metaphor for a prepublished text written on a computer should not obscure the fact that handwritten texts are not the same as printed texts. Manuscripts have an altogether different relationship to other written texts (including other copies of the same text) and an altogether different social value and function than printed texts (see Johnson 2010). *See* chirograph.

MEDIA CRITICISM

The analysis of the function and dynamics of various media of communication (speech, writing, ritual, etc.), and especially of the significance of shifts from one medium to another (e.g. from oral to written expression).

MEDIA MIX
The distribution of and interrelationships between various media of communication within society. The term "media mix" helps media critics remember and account for the simultaneous presence of multiple communicative media and to avoid treating them as mutually exclusive phenomena. *See* Great Divide, the.

MEDIUM
A mode of communication, including spoken word, ritual act, written text, inscribed object, etc. Kelber refers to "the modalities of language," which he lists as "oral, chirographic, typographic, and electronic" (1983:21), though human cultures exhibit more than just these four media.

MEMORY
The recall, representation, and interpretation of the perceived past. For helpful introductory discussions of memory—especially "social" or "collective" memory—among NT scholars, see Kirk and Thatcher 2005; Allison 2010:1–17; Rodríguez 2010:41–80.

MEMORIZATION
The fixing of a story or text (and especially the *words* of the story or text) in memory, so that the story is retold in exactly the same way in multiple performances. Many oral traditions include a claim to verbatim stability, but closer investigation reveals considerable variability in different accounts of the same tradition (i.e. the story is recognizably similar rather than exactly the same). Nevertheless, some traditions are memorized verbatim. As a result, scholars have found it helpful to maintain a distinction between memorization and memory.

METONYMY
"[A] mode of signification wherein the part stands for the whole" (Foley 1991:7), or "*pars pro toto* signification" (Foley 1995a:48). The individual words, phrases, and even themes of a traditional work tap into meanings and associations larger than their strictly literal or denotative meaning. In a traditional register, words communicate "extra information" because, within that register, they have been associated with that information in previous performances. *See* economy, communicative; *pars pro toto*; register; traditional referentiality.

MNEMOHISTORY

An area of historical research that focuses on the question of how people and societies remember the past rather than the question of what really happened. According to German Egyptologist Jan Assmann, who coined the term "mnemohistory," "Unlike history proper, mnemohistory is concerned not with the past as such, but only with the past as it is remembered. . . . Mnemohistory is reception theory applied to history" (1997:8–9).

MODALITY

See medium.

MOUVANCE

Developed by French medievalist Paul Zumthor, *mouvance* refers to the variability or instability of manuscripts/chirographs. Media critics insist that *mouvance* is not a corrupting influence on manuscripts, as though the text of the "original" manuscript was being degraded or corrupted in the process of transmission (= hand-copying). Instead, *mouvance* is a key feature of tradition expressed in handwritten media; manuscript tradition is authentically and fundamentally equiprimordial, multiform, and plural (see Kirk 2008:225–34). One helpful way to account for *mouvance* is to distinguish a manuscript tradition from the actual, concrete texts that embody that tradition (e.g. the manuscript tradition of the Gospel of Matthew, as distinct from the individual extant manuscript copies of Matthew).[2] *See* chirograph; equiprimordiality; manuscript; multiformity; plurality; Tradition.

MULTIFORMITY

The idea that a tradition exists in multiple forms at the same time, so that no one form of the tradition represents a more "authentic" or "original" form of that tradition. *See* equiprimordiality; *mouvance*; plurality.

ORAL-DERIVED TEXT

A broad spectrum of written texts "that either stem directly from or have roots in oral tradition" (Foley 1991:xi). Foley offers a four-fold typology of oral-derived texts, ranging from Oral Performance, Voiced Texts, Voices from the Past, and on to Written Oral Poems (see Chapter Four).

ORAL-FORMULAIC THEORY

An approach to the language and structure of oral epic as well as of traditional texts suspected to be composed-in-performance. Developed by Homeric scholars Milman Parry and Albert Lord, the Oral-Formulaic Theory identifies the formula as the essential building block of orally composed epic. Parry and Lord identified significant similarities between South Slavic oral epics, which they recorded in the early twentieth century, and the Homeric *Iliad* and the *Odyssey*. Since Parry and Lord could witness the oral composition-in-performance of South Slavic oral epics, and since the language of those oral epics resembled the language of the *Iliad* and the *Odyssey*, they concluded that the Homeric texts must have been composed under similar conditions (i.e. orally). *See* composition-in-performance; economy; formula.

ORAL RESIDUE

The persistent influence of oral psychodynamics in a literate culture (see Ong 1982:36, 37, *passim*). *See* orality, residual; psychodynamics.

ORAL SYNTHESIS

A concept developed by Werner Kelber (1983) that highlights the fusion of speaker, message (or text), and audience in oral performance. The theory of oral synthesis emphasizes the connection between knowledge and the person/people who embody and/or communicate that knowledge; "oral cultures have great difficulty in separating the knower from the known" (Kelber 1983:147, citing Ong 1978:109).

ORAL TEXT

1 The verbal content of an oral performance, especially one that does not involve any written text or script. *See* performance.

2 A written text that demonstrates an "oral/aural character" (Graham 1987:36). This meaning of "oral text" assumes that orality exhibits certain stable characteristics that are distinct from the psychodynamics of writing. So when a written text exhibits oral characteristics, scholars refer to it as an "oral text." *See* homeostasis; orality; psychodynamics.

ORALITY

The quality of being oral (as opposed to *textuality*, "the quality of being written"). The term "orality" was coined in order to avoid the value-laden connotations of literacy's usual opposite, "illiteracy." However, "orality" has come to refer to a number of other things in addition to "being oral." Researchers variously use "orality" to refer to certain stylistic features (e.g. repetition, chiasm, etc.), to certain cultural features (e.g. the lack of writing and/or written texts, egalitarian power structures, etc.), or even certain value judgments (e.g. the virtue of preindustrial societies *vis-à-vis* modern capitalist Western societies). Prominent British cultural anthropologist Ruth Finnegan concludes: "in one sense 'orality' is *not* anything: or at any rate not anything in the apparently unitary sense that the term seems to imply" (Finnegan 1990:146; see also Rodríguez 2009). For an example of this "apparently unitary sense," Pieter Botha refers to "the oral-aural mindset" (1993b:421), though nowhere has he clearly and concretely defined that mindset.

ORALITY, PRIMARY

Orality before the acquisition of literacy skills within a given culture. Walter Ong refers to the orality "of persons totally unfamiliar with writing" and, beyond the individual, "of a culture totally untouched by any knowledge of writing or print" (1982:6, 10). *See* orality.

ORALITY, RESIDUAL

The persistence of oral psychodynamics during the ascendance of literate psychodynamics. Walter Ong refers to "habits of thought and expression tracing back to preliterate situations or practice, or deriving from the dominance of the oral as a medium in a given culture, or indicating a reluctance or inability to dissociate the written medium from the spoken" (1971:25–6). *See* orality; psychodynamics.

ORALITY, SECONDARY

1 Orality after the acquisition of literacy skills within a given culture. Walter Ong refers to "an orality not antecedent to writing and print, as primary orality is, but consequent upon and dependent upon writing and print" (1982:167). Secondary orality in this sense depends upon the presence and influence of writing and print media. Examples of this kind of secondary orality include electronic media, digital recordings, etc.

2 Among biblical scholars, "secondary orality" often refers to "indirect familiarity with texts through oral tradition" (Goodacre

2012:137), or, in other words, the "re-oralization" of written tradition (see Kelber 1983:217–18). This second use of "secondary orality" is often regarded as incorrect or, at best, unhelpful (see Young 2011:104, n. 123).

Parataxis
Placing simple sentences alongside one another (Greek *para* (alongside) + *tassein* (to order)) by means of a coordinating conjunction (and, but, for, etc.) rather than a subordinating conjunction (after, since, in order that, etc.).

Pars pro toto
"Part for the whole." *See* economy, communicative; immanence; Immanent Art; metonymy.

Performance
The social event (or experience) within which a performer enacts a tradition, whether by telling it orally from memory or reading from a written text, and in which an audience experiences that tradition. Media critics highlight performance for a couple of reasons, including (1) to emphasize that the traditions we are analyzing were experienced as multi-sensory events rather than two-dimensional texts, and (2) to explore how other modes of experience affect the meaning and impact of these traditions (see Rhoads 2006a:2–3). Richard Bauman identifies performance as "an aesthetically marked and heightened mode of communication, framed in a special way and put on display for an audience" (1992b:41, cited by Maxey 2009:85). *See* Immanent Art.

Performance arena
1 The place where oral performance takes place, "where words are invested with their special power. . . . a recurrent forum dedicated to a specific kind of activity, a defined and defining site in which enactment can occur again and again without devolution into a repetitive, solely chronological series" (Foley 1995a:47; see 47–9). For actual oral performances, the performance arena refers to a physical location—the site of the event—including especially any ritualistic aspects of the site.

2 The "place" in which readers and/or audiences imagine themselves as they read and/or experience an oral-derived text. An audience experienced with the actual oral tradition of an oral-derived text can summon the memory of the actual space of the

performance arena in their reception of the oral-derived text. But for inexperienced audiences, an oral-derived text must signal its performance arena rhetorically: "the 'place' where the work is experienced by a reader, the event that is re-created, must be summoned solely by textual signals" (Foley 1995a:80; see 79–82). As text and audience become further removed from the text's oral tradition, the presence and consequence of the performance arena for the text's reception become increasingly irrelevant. *See* Immanent Art.

PERFORMANCE THEORY
A critical approach for analyzing NT texts and traditions that "highlights the social, cultural, and aesthetic dimensions of the communicative process" (Bauman 1992b:41, cited by Maxey 2009:85). Performance theory involves transposing the written texts of the NT into an event. Ideally, the newly reconstituted event bears some relation to early Christian performances of NT tradition, though we can never really know whether this is true. However, performance criticism does bring into sharp relief the artificiality of our experiences of private, silent reading of texts and traditions that were originally experienced orally and communally.

PLURALITY
The principle according to which multiple versions of an utterance, story, or tradition are authentic, independent, and unique. "Because every oral performance draws its meaning and energy from its own peculiar biosphere (a unique social context and moment), three very similar renderings of a traditional saying should be viewed as three completely autonomous texts" (Thatcher 2008:5; Thatcher uses the term "biosphere" using meaning no. 2, above). *See* biosphere; equiprimordiality; multiformity.

PROSODY
The stress, rhythm, intonation, pace, and other paralinguistic features of oral communication. Prosodic features of oral speech have dramatic—even determinative—consequences for the reception and interpretation of verbal messages. As an everyday example, the message, "Thank you," can communicate either gratitude or ingratitude, and it can do so without any additional verbal information. Differences in tone, posture, body language (e.g. rolling one's eyes), volume, and so on easily make clear

whether "Thank you" means, "I owe you one," or "That was completely useless."

PSYCHODYNAMICS

Walter Ong (and those influenced by him) use the term "psychodynamics" to refer to characteristics of thought and expression. Theorists such as Ong, Eric Havelock, and Jack Goody argue that communications media have characteristic patterns of thought that distinguish each medium from others. Therefore, Ong refers to characteristics that "set off orally based thought and expression from chirographically and typographically based thought and expression" (1982:36; see 36–57). Use of this term among media critics easily devolves into assuming the "Great Divide" theory of communicative media, since media critics who use this term imply (or explicitly claim) that orality and literacy have distinctive and unique cognitive, social, and cultural characteristics. *See* Great Divide, the.

REGISTER

The "special language," whether oral or written, dedicated to expressing a particular subject or type of subject. With respect to the questions of oral tradition and the NT, the term "register" refers to the linguistic features deemed appropriate for expressing the Jesus tradition, communicating across expanded distances by written letters, and so on. The key feature of a distinctive traditional register, however, is not its unique words, phrases, and expressions, but rather the "institutionalized meanings" conveyed by means of those words, phrases, and expressions (see Foley 1995a:49–53). *See* immanence; Immanent Art.

REPETITION

The recurrence of words, phrases, and themes that "proves not just a typical but a constitutive dimension of many oral traditional registers" (Foley 1995a:90). Repetition in "nontraditional" texts often comes across as dull and uncreative. In traditional texts, however, linguistic and narrative repetitions "represent the inevitable products of a consistent, rule-governed process rather than recycled items from a limited inventory" (Foley 2002:137).

SCRIBALITY

The medium of handwritten texts, including the associated social, cultural, and ideological aspects of that medium (e.g. the social function[s] and/or cultural significance[s] of handwritten texts, or the political control over the production, possession, and deployment of handwritten texts).

SCRIPT
A written text that exists before an oral performance and enables that performance. *See* transcript.

TEXT-FIXATION
See entextualization.

TEXTUALITY
1 The quality of being written (as opposed to *orality*, "the quality of being oral").

2 The use of written texts for rhetorical, political, or social purposes, whether or not someone actually reads the texts, strictly speaking. Historian Brian Stock distinguishes "literacy" (which requires the ability to read written texts) from "textuality." This distinction provides a way for us to appreciate that "illiterate people can have comparatively robust access to textual traditions and can utilize them to conduct their affairs and pursue their interests" (Rodríguez 2009:164; see Stock 1983:7). The very many references to Jesus teaching, interpreting, and debating the Hebrew Bible with the scribes, Pharisees, Sadducees, and other Jews of Roman-era Judea and Galilee provide useful illustrations of the concept of textuality because, with the exception of Lk 4.16–21, Jesus is never depicted as actually reading a written text (see Rodríguez 2010:152–65; Keith 2011a).[3]

THRIFT
See economy.

TRADENT
Someone who recounts the tradition, whether orally or in writing.

TRADITION
A body of established, inherited patterns of speech, behavior, thought, social organization, and so on. John Miles Foley defines "tradition" as "a dynamic, multivalent *body of meaning*" (1995a:xii; emphasis added) and repeatedly refers to tradition as the "enabling referent" that allows a specific oral text or oral-derived text to facilitate communication between a performer (or reader) and an audience. He goes on to identify tradition as "a living and vital

entity with synchronic and diachronic aspects that over time and space will experience (and partially constitute) a unified variety of receptions" (1995a:xii). *See* Immanent Art.

TRADITIONAL REFERENTIALITY

The idea that the meaning (or reference) of traditional words and phrases remains relatively stable across multiple performances and even performers. Traditional referentiality requires the fluent engagement of both text and context by the performer and audience (in the case of an oral performance) or the author and reader (in the case of an oral-derived text) to access and appreciate the metonymic significance of traditional language (see Foley 1991:6–8). *See* economy, communicative; immanence; Immanent Art; metonymy.

TRANSCRIPT

A written text that exists after an oral performance and documents the wording of that performance. *See* script.

WORD

"[A] unit of utterance, an irreducible atom of performance, a speech-act" (Foley 2002:13). Foley goes on to describe a word as "a sound-byte, a distinct and *integral unit of expression*" (2002:14; emphasis added). This expanded definition of "word" cautions against focusing narrowly or exclusively on the individual lexical units of our written texts ("words" in the normal sense) and to think in terms of whole, integral units of communication—words, phrases, themes, and stories.

WORD POWER

The ability of traditional words, phrases, and themes to transcend their textual, denotative significance and engage their contextualizing tradition efficiently and effectively (see Foley 1995a).

CHAPTER THREE

The *who* of oral tradition and NT studies

The eighteenth-century German philosopher Johann Gottfried Herder (1744–1803) is often credited as the first critic to propose seriously an oral source behind the Gospels. Intensive efforts to account for and recover pre-Gospel oral tradition, however, began in earnest in the early twentieth century (see Mournet 2005:3–7). In 1919 Martin Dibelius published *From Tradition to Gospel*,[1] and two years later Rudolf Bultmann published the first edition of his seminal work, *The History of the Synoptic Tradition*.[2] Dibelius and Bultmann, together with Karl Schmidt,[3] gave rise to *Formgeschichte*, which is typically translated "form criticism" (see Tucker 2010). The form critics focused especially on the *origins* and the *development* of the pre-Gospel oral tradition. As a result, they pursued an inherently source-critical agenda, inquiring after both the sources of the oral Jesus tradition and the oral sources of our written Gospels (e.g. Dibelius 1935:v).

Contemporary biblical media criticism frequently begins with the form critics, and rightly so.[4] However, as I will argue over the course of this and the next chapters, the form critics got us started on the wrong foot. We have not simply advanced *beyond* the original contributions of Dibelius and Bultmann. We have begun to ask *fundamentally different questions* from those that arrested the attention of the form critics. Contemporary media criticism is, in many ways, a reaction against twentieth-century form criticism.

However, contemporary media criticism offers more than a negative reaction against the form critics; it also offers a positive vision of Christian origins and the interpretation of the NT texts. Since our focus is on this positive vision, we will begin our historical survey with the post-form-critical study of oral tradition and the NT. (For a survey of the form critics' views on oral tradition, specifically those of Bultmann and Dibelius, see Mournet 2005:55–63.)

Birger Gerhardsson

A logical place to begin the history of contemporary media criticism is with Swedish scholar Birger Gerhardsson. His dissertation, *Memory and Manuscript* (1961), was published at the zenith of form criticism's influence, when the academic community was not ready to take seriously Gerhardsson's critical challenges to form criticism.[5] Gerhardsson's work would not be granted adequate consideration for at least two decades, and perhaps closer to four. Perhaps most (in)famously, Morton Smith wrote an influential and dismissive review essay that described Gerhardsson's thesis as a whole as "impossible to conceive" (1963:176). Two decades later, Werner Kelber (1983) would take Gerhardsson seriously, and 15 years after that, in 1998, Gerhardsson's book would be republished, along with his follow-up essay, *Tradition and Transmission in Early Christianity* (1964), and a penitent foreword by no less than esteemed Rabbinics scholar (and Morton Smith's former student) Jacob Neusner. Finally, in 2009, an edited volume of interdisciplinary essays would reassess the original significance of Gerhardsson's work (Kelber and Byrskog 2009). Today, Gerhardsson is widely recognized as a seminal figure in the history of research in early Christian oral tradition, a man literally decades ahead of his time.

Gerhardsson has maintained a consistent focus on the *transmission* of oral tradition throughout his publishing career. His primary disagreement with the form critics concerns the transmission of the tradition (1961:14). He begins by lodging a complaint against the form critics' "lack of clarity" about the transmission of oral tradition among the early Christians, and he sets out "to determine what was the technical procedure followed when the early Church *transmitted*, both gospel and other material" (14–15; emphasis in the original). Toward this end, Gerhardsson carefully analyzes the transmission of both the written and the oral Torah in Rabbinic Judaism (33–70, 71–189, respectively). Jacob Neusner interprets Gerhardsson's comparative intentions perhaps too graciously, claiming that Gerhardsson "does not claim in these pages to know how the oral traditions of any Judaism were formulated and transmitted before A.D. 70" (1998:xxv). In actual fact, Gerhardsson appeals to examples from "Tannaitic and Amoraic times"—that is, the first through fifth-centuries CE (1961:56)—to justify his thesis about Jesus in the 20s or 30s of the first-century CE. That is, Jesus "must have made his disciples learn certain sayings off by heart; if he taught, he must have required his disciples to memorize. This statement is not intended to be dogmatic or apologetic but is a consideration based on *a comparison with the contemporary situation*" (56, 328; my emphasis).[6] Gerhardsson continues to employ the analogy with Rabbinic Judaism, insisting that the Rabbinic analogy helps explain both the kind of teacher Jesus was and the kind of students the disciples were (305–6; 2005:9).

The form critics too often assumed that the Gospels and the pre-Gospel oral tradition had no historical connection to the actual life and ministry of Jesus. Gerhardsson, in contrast, rightly recognized that the early Christians thought they were passing on Jesus' actual teachings and accounts of his actual life. According to Gerhardsson, Jesus' disciples preserved his teaching by committing it to memory and transmitting his teaching in memorized form (1961:329). This recognition alone represents a significant advance over NT scholarship's form-critical legacy (similarly, see Bauckham 2006). However, Gerhardsson goes too far when he argues, on the basis of both the Acts of the Apostles and Paul's letters, that the disciples—specifically, The Twelve—formed a *collegium*, or authoritative school, that was responsible for forming, preserving, and transmitting the Jesus tradition (1961:244, 245–61).[7]

In the course of the present investigation we have come to the conclusion that the leading *collegium* in the Jerusalem church carried out a direct work on *ho logos tou kyriou* (i.e. the Holy Scriptures and the tradition from, and about, Christ). From certain points of view this work resembled the labours of Rabbinic Judaism on *dabar* YHWH (the Holy Scriptures and the oral Torah) and the work carried out in the Qumran congregation of *dabar* YHWH (the Holy Scriptures and the sect's own tradition, which was partly oral and partly written). This apostolic work on "the word of God" was thus the most important element in the comprehensive concept *hē didachē tōn apostolōn* (Acts 2.42) and the concept *hē diakonia tou logou* (Acts 6.4). (331).

This *collegium*—and "the young Church" (1961: *passim*) in general—developed and transmitted a fixed tradition of Jesus' teachings, which tradition "was partly memorized and partly written down in notebooks and private scrolls" (335).

All of this rests on a highly speculative reading of a handful of texts, especially Acts 15 (see 249–61). For example, he calls Acts 15.5ff. "a description of a *regular* early Christian general session" (251; emphasis added), though nothing in Acts 15 (or elsewhere) suggests that it describes a regular or recurring kind of meeting. Instead, Acts 15 seems to describe a special, ad hoc gathering of the Jerusalem church to settle a significant, persistent problem that was not typical for the early Christians. Moreover, Paul's letters provide authoritative doctrinal and pragmatic pronouncements to their audiences from Paul himself *and not from Jerusalem*. This fact alone suggests that authority among the earliest Christians was not concentrated in a small group located in Jerusalem. But the bigger problem is that Gerhardsson moves too easily from the observation that the traditions of Jesus' teachings and activities were "isolated" to the assumption that that isolated Jesus tradition was "memorized," or fixed at the level of its wording. When Gerhardsson describes the tradition of Jesus' teaching as "isolated," he means that the earliest Christians kept Jesus' *teachings* separate from the *functions* for which they used those teachings (see 334–5; 2001:59–63).

Gerhardsson's conception of the oral Jesus tradition, then, is too rigid and inflexible, especially in that he assumes a fixed oral tradition that was more stable and unchanging than even the written Jesus tradition![8] To be sure, Gerhardsson leaves room for the adaptation and creative application of the fixed Jesus tradition in earliest Christianity. But the Jesus tradition as Gerhardsson has imagined it is nevertheless unreasonably and impractically stable, fixed, and memorized.

Werner H. Kelber

Birger Gerhardsson offered real advances over the form critics because he offered a historically grounded model for the transmission of the oral Jesus tradition. Two decades later, Werner Kelber advanced the discussion once again by appealing to important work that had been done in other fields (outside biblical scholarship) on communications media, culture, and tradition. Kelber's work bears the influence of two men in particular: cultural historian Walter Ong, and oral traditionalist Albert Lord. Kelber takes seriously the notion that the medium of communication (oral, handwritten, printed, or electronic) affects the production and reception of a message or text. When his book was reissued in 1997, Kelber explained his approach in terms of "the polarity of orality versus textuality" (xxi). That is, Kelber rejected the general assumption of the form critics that the oral Jesus tradition evolved steadily into the form we see in the written Gospels. Instead, Kelber argues that the written Gospel of Mark actually disrupts the pre-Gospel oral tradition and transforms it into something else:

> Mark's writing project is an act of daring and rife with consequences. To the extent that the gospel draws on oral voices, it has rendered them voiceless. The voiceprints of once-spoken words have been muted. This is an extraordinary undertaking. . . . The text, while asserting itself out of dominant oral traditions and activities, has brought about a freezing of oral life into textual still life. (1983:91)

Despite Kelber's protest that he never used the phrase "Great Divide" to describe the relation between oral and textual expressions of tradition (e.g. Kelber and Thatcher 2008:29–30), scholars have found this very perspective in Kelber's work, and for good reason.[9]

In *The Oral and the Written Gospel*, Kelber argued two primary points. First, the oral contexts in which early Christians told stories of Jesus affected the production, content, structure, and function of written texts (the Gospel of Mark, Paul's letters, etc.). Kelber speaks of "Mark's indebtedness to oral life and nonliterate consciousness," he assumes "an importation of oral features into the [written] gospel," and he finds it reasonable to expect that "oral forms and conventions will . . . have gained admittance into the written document" (1983:44). Kelber devotes an entire chapter to exploring "Mark's oral legacy" (44–89) and ultimately concludes that the Gospel of Mark preserves evidence of the pre-Gospel "unorganized oral lore" (79) in its individual parts but not in its overall narrative form.[10]

Kelber's second primary point, on the other hand, drives a sharp wedge between the written Gospel of Mark and the pre-Gospel oral tradition. Here Kelber speaks of "Mark's disruption of the oral lifeworld" and argues that the act of transposing the pre-Gospel oral stories into a written narrative creates "a novel unity" (91). If the individual parts of Mark's Gospel preserve traces of the oral Jesus tradition, the author of Mark nevertheless "chose the written medium, *not to recapitulate oral messages, but to transform them*" (130; emphasis added). If we step back from these two points, we can make two general observations. First, Kelber agrees with the form critics in thinking of the pre-Gospel oral tradition as the individual story-units of the Gospel (healing and exorcism stories, parables, controversy stories, etc.). Second, he disagrees with the form critics' view of the written Gospel as a natural or logical extension of the oral Jesus tradition. In other words, in some very important ways Kelber agrees with the form critics about the *oral* Jesus tradition, but he disagrees with them about the *written* Jesus tradition.

But this is an oversimplification, and Kelber has offered some real advances over the form critics' conceptualization of the oral Jesus tradition in his later publications. I will focus on two such advances, both from his essay, "Jesus and Tradition: Words in Time, Words in Space" (1995). First, Kelber developed further the notion of the oral Jesus tradition's multiformity. He recognized that Jesus himself (not just the early Christians) could utter the same saying or tell the same parable in different ways on different occasions. Jesus' teaching itself "occurred in multiformity that was tantamount to multioriginality. A thrice-narrated parable was not comprehensible in terms of a core structure and three variables thereof, but only as three equiprimordial renditions. Each rendition was an original version, and in fact *the original version*" (151; italics in the original). Kelber goes too far—that is, he speaks too strongly—when he attributes originality to *every* oral utterance. In other words, *equi*primordial says too much. However, he rightly broadens our thinking beyond *the* (singular) original form of a saying or tradition. His emphasis on equiprimordiality pushes us to acknowledge a plurality of authentically original, genuine versions of a saying or group of sayings, or "the oral implementation of multioriginality in the present act of speaking" (162).

Second, Kelber offered a brilliant (if awkward) metaphor of tradition as a "biosphere" that provided a total context for any given expression of tradition.

> If we conceive of tradition as a more inclusive and less tangible reality than our literate senses let us know, we must also consider the role of hearers. . . . [I]n order to grasp the fuller implications of hearers' participation (not simply responses!), we will in the end have to overcome our textbound thinking and come to terms with *a reality that is not encoded in texts at all*. It means that we must learn to think of *a large part of tradition as an extratextual phenomenon*. . . . Tradition in this encompassing sense is a circumambient contextuality or biosphere in which speaker and hearers live. It includes texts and experiences transmitted through or derived from texts. But it is anything but reducible to intertextuality. Tradition in this broadest sense is largely *an invisible nexus of references and identities* from which people draw sustenance, in which they live, and in relation to which they make sense of their lives. *This invisible biosphere is at once the most elusive and the foundational feature of tradition.* (159; emphases added)

With the metaphor of tradition as biosphere, Kelber begins to leave behind the form-critical conception of oral tradition in favor of viewing oral tradition as a *context* of communication rather than simply as a *medium* of communication. Kelber recognized that *oral tradition*, as an analytical concept, encompassed much more than simply another source lurking behind our extant written texts, like Q or *Ur-Markus*, and this was his major innovation.[11] In light of the explosion of the influence of media-critical scholarship since 1983, we exaggerate only slightly if we speak of a "Kelber Revolution" in NT scholarship.[12]

Joanna Dewey

Since the beginning of her publishing career, Joanna Dewey has consistently focused on the structure of Mark's Gospel (see Dewey 1973, 1980). In 1989, she began focusing on the structure of Mark's Gospel in light of its oral composition and reception. In direct response to the thesis that Mark's Gospel amounts to a "textually induced eclipse of voices and sound" (Kelber 1983:91), Dewey argues that "Mark *as a whole*—not just its individual episodes—shows the legacy of orality, indeed that its methods of composition are primarily oral ones" (1989:33; emphasis in the original). In other words, Dewey comes very close to identifying the whole Gospel of Mark as oral Jesus tradition.

Dewey works with a Great Divide conception of oral and written expressions of tradition (see Dewey 2008:86). In her analysis, oral tradition and written tradition are two separate and separable things. They might exist side-by-side in certain cultural environments, but they relate to each other like oil and water. Dewey refers to the cultural environment in which Mark was written and read as "a manuscript culture with high residual orality," a culture that exhibited "considerable overlap between orality and textuality" (1989:33). The Gospel of Mark, as a written text, participated in the culture's emerging "textuality," but its composition and its reception are both influenced by its ongoing influence from "orality." Accordingly, Dewey concludes that certain features of the written text suggest that the Gospel "was composed for a listening, not a reading, audience," including Mark's emphasis on events rather than discourse, its paratactic structure, and other alleged oral characteristics. If the Gospel of Mark was composed orally and incorporates oral features, then "we need to take the dynamics of orality much more seriously in interpreting the Gospel of Mark and in reconstructing early Christian history" (see 34–42).

You might notice a strong element of circularity here. Dewey describes certain elements (repetition, parataxis, etc.) as "oral," then finds these elements in a written text (which might have suggested to another critic that these elements were not necessarily oral after all). Then, she concludes that readers of this particular written text need to pay closer attention to the "orality" that she has detected within the written text. But we have only Dewey's word (and her references to Walter Ong and Eric Havelock) to guarantee that these are actually features of orality and that their presence in the written text of Mark is foreign to that text's medium of communication (i.e. its textuality).[13] This circularity may provide the necessary explanation for how Dewey can say, almost 20 years later, that this particular written text, *despite being a written text*, "remains fundamentally on the oral side of the oral/written divide" (2008:86).

In 1991 Dewey published a media-critical analysis of Mark's narrative structure. She argues that Mark does not follow a linear, logical structure that lends itself to developing a singular thesis. Linear, logical narrative structures, of course, are characteristics of written texts rather than of oral texts like Mark. Rather than a linear narrative, Mark "is an interwoven tapestry or fugue made up of multiple overlapping structures and sequences, forecasts of what is to come and echoes of what has already been said" (1991:224). This structure, again, is alien to Mark's medium of communication; "such nonlinear recursive compositional style is characteristic of aural narrative" (i.e. narrative intended to be *heard* rather than *read*; 224). Dewey then proceeds to identify the various ways Mark has woven together his "tapestry or fugue":

> Interconnections, or repetitions and anticipations, are anything and everything that remind a hearer of other parts of the narrative. A list of the ways episodes or series of episodes can be interconnected would include theme, manifest content, particular aspects of content such as setting, geography, or characters, form-critical type, and rhetorical devices such as key and hook words, inclusios, intercalations and frames, parallel and chiastic repetitions. (225)

None of these "interconnections" requires an oral medium to make sense as structural markers.[14] But of course they do not. We were always analyzing a written text, and these methods of interconnection function perfectly naturally within the written medium. The only connection between structure and medium is Dewey's persistent reference to such links as "oral methods of narrative development" (234), usually with a reference to Ong or Havelock near to hand.

In 1995, Dewey introduced the question of power relations into her theory of communications media. In "Textuality in an Oral

Culture," she argues, "Christianity began as an oral phenomenon in a predominantly oral culture within which the dominant elite were literate and made extensive use of writing to maintain hegemony and control" (1995:38). In other words, Dewey maps a second "great divide" (common people vs ruling elite) onto her first great divide (orality vs textuality). Moreover, she draws a sharp contrast between the egalitarian social harmony of the oral common folk and the domineering exercise of power by the literate ruling elite.[15] Other scholars have also raised the question of the relationship between literacy, written texts, authority, and the exercise of power, especially Richard Horsley (see below). However, many of these analyses fail to recognize that illiterate groups are not automatically or even usually egalitarian communities. People manage to create and enforce unequal power relationships even without the use of written texts, a fact for which Dewey fails to take sufficient account. Moreover, illiterate populations often manage to navigate a world with robust textual influences *despite* their inability to read literary texts. This certainly applies to the social worlds of the NT. The discussion in the next two chapters, therefore, will need to provide greater nuance and precision in how we conceive of power, literacy, and the interaction between the two.

Paul J. Achtemeier

One year after Joanna Dewey's initial foray into media criticism and Mark's Gospel, Paul Achtemeier published a significant essay on reading aloud in the Roman era. In "*Omne Verbum Sonat*," Achtemeier focuses narrowly on "indications in written documents that would make their oral performance understandable even in the absence of any rhetorical training on the part of the writer or the listener" (1990:9). Achtemeier, like Kelber, exhibits considerable influence from Walter Ong, especially Ong's notion that "more than any other single invention, writing has transformed human consciousness" (Ong 1982:79; cited in Achtemeier 1990:4). Therefore, Achtemeier begins by demonstrating "a cultural bias in favor of the oral over the written" in late Western antiquity (9–10), a bias that was facilitated in part by "the sheer physical nature of the written page in classical antiquity" (10–11). Despite the wide range of materials used for writing, and the broad range of functions for the written word, late Western antiquity retained an "essential orality . . . demonstrated both in the manner by which literature was produced and in the manner in which it was read. Both were predominantly, indeed exclusively, oral" (12). That is, literature was produced by dictation,[16] and it was read by recitation[17] (see 12–17).

Achtemeier has made his point too strongly, and we will have to undo some of his influence over NT media criticism. A number of studies since 1990 have presented serious challenges to the view that reading (to say nothing of writing) was always done aloud.[18] His essay nevertheless remains important for two reasons. First, even though the main thrust of his argument has been discredited, scholars continue to cite Achtemeier as the definitive authority substantiating the claim that reading in antiquity was reading aloud. New Testament scholarship needs to recognize and acknowledge that Achtemeier was simply wrong.[19]

Second, and more importantly, Achtemeier's essay rightly senses that reading, as a cultural activity, varies from culture to culture. A whole range of factors affect how people read written texts and what broader social or cultural significance people attach to the act of reading. Questions include: What kinds of information get written down? What kinds of situations might include reading from a written text (religious, political, economic, educational, etc.)? Who is permitted to read the texts, and what ceremonial procedures are lectors expected to follow? What kinds of authority do people attribute to the contents of the written text? What kinds of authority do people attribute to the written text itself? What expectations do people bring to the act of reading, and what consequences follow if a lector fails to uphold those expectations? How does a culture format its written texts to facilitate its cultural needs? And so on. Achtemeier's essay does not raise and address these questions, but it does prepare us to expect and to look for culturally specific dynamics of reading.

Pieter J. J. Botha

South African NT scholar Pieter Botha has consistently focused his attention on the culturally specific practices of writing and reading since his 1990 essay, "Mute Manuscripts: Analysing a Neglected

Aspect of Ancient Communication." Botha rightly recognizes that "[c]ommunication media not only *reflect* culture but also *influence* it fundamentally. Writing is a socially determined phenomenon" (1990:35; italics in the original). In other words, the technologies of writing and reading are not transcultural constants that manifest themselves in the same or even similar ways in every culture. In "Mute Manuscripts" Botha explicitly sets out to oppose this idea: "The thesis of this paper is that an unrecognized assumption underlies most exegetical activities, namely that writing implies a *constant* role and/or function in communication" (39; italics in the original).

To these ends, Botha offers brief discussions of orality, literacy, and scribal culture (39–42). Interestingly enough, Botha provides basic definitions of both "literacy" and "scribal culture,"[20] but one looks in vain for a similar definition of "orality." To be sure, we find a number of descriptors: "spoken discourse is not yet orality. . . . Orality, as a condition, exists by virtue of communication that is not dependent on modern media processes and techniques. It is negatively formed by the lack of technology and positively created by specific forms of education and cultural activities" (40). But none of these comments tell readers what orality *is*. The closest we come to a definition comes a few sentences later: "Orality refers to the experience of words (and speech) in the habitat of sound" (40), but readers would be forgiven for wanting a more concrete definition.[21] I offer this as a sympathetic criticism; Botha has inherited the concept of orality from others (especially Walter Ong, but also Eric Havelock and Jack Goody) without appreciating its lack of substance and specificity.

Consequently, Botha can only loosely describe the connection between "orality" (whatever that is) and the actual manuscripts of the ancient world. Nevertheless, he rightly recognizes that, at least in some cases, we need to carefully examine some concepts that we take for granted. For example, I think we ought to apply Botha's description of "authorship" to the four canonical Gospels: "[Authors] pursued and performed instructional functions for their community, fulfilling an essential role as *agents and instruments of the oral tradition and cultural experience*" (42–3; emphasis added). The written texts of the Gospels embody and express the Jesus tradition rather than the creative genius of the Evangelists. This is not the form-critical notion that the Gospels are community products rather than the work of an individual author.[22] Media critics acknowledge that some performers of the tradition are more fluent in the traditional register than others. Some performances of the tradition activate the tradition's potential more effectively than others. In light of the apparently positive reception of the Gospels among the earliest Christians, including their eventual inclusion in the Christian canon, media criticism enables us to recognize both the Evangelists' authorial—or better, performative—achievement as well as their situatedness within the biosphere of the early Jesus tradition. Botha consistently attempts to situate the NT authors (especially the Evangelists, but also Paul) within a more appropriate reconstruction of first-century CE Mediterranean culture.

The next year, Botha published an article on the transmission of tradition and the composition of Mark's Gospel (Botha 1991). When Botha calls the Gospel of Mark "traditional," he is referring to "the composition *technique* described by the oral formulaic theory" (307; italics in the original). That is, Botha is proposing that Mark was composed-in-performance under the constraints of rapid, extemporaneous speaking in the presence of a live audience (see 308).[23] The Markan account of Jesus' life and teaching was not memorized, but it was told from memory, "with slight variations at various performances, and *the text as we now have it* is but an instance, a reflection of one performance of that traditional *process*" (307; italics in the original). Botha spends a considerable part of this essay summarizing the Oral-Formulaic Theory, both its main components and some possible objections (see 307–17). He then briefly describes Mark's "formulaic style" (317–19) and "thematic composition" (319–22), both of which confirm, for Botha, that Mark is an oral traditional text. "So it is quite possible that the Gospel of Mark is a casual transcription of what had been performed orally" (322). In other words, the Markan tradition of Jesus' life and teaching was repeatedly expressed in oral performances before live audiences, and the written text of Mark's Gospel reflects the whole of this oral tradition rather than the oral text of any one single performance.

Botha does not restrict his attention to the Gospels. Like Werner Kelber, who devoted an entire chapter to "orality and textuality in Paul" (1983:140–83), Botha also turns his media-critical gaze toward Paul's letters (1992 and 1993b). He begins in much the same way as this book began: by chronicling the relative scarcity of literacy in antiquity and the largely illiterate condition of both Greco-Roman and Hellenistic-Jewish cultures in the first century. This large-scale illiteracy affects the social function of Paul's (written) letters, even though certainly Paul and/or his amanuensis were literate. "It is important to bear in mind that even the literates were literate in an illiterate culture. Orality (in a cultural-anthropological sense) and the social effects of illiteracy permeate even their 'literate' communication" (1992:19–21; 20–1 quoted).[24]

Understandably, then, Botha emphasizes the oral-performative nature of both the composition and the delivery of Paul's letters. He develops a point that commentators often note but rarely account for, namely, that almost all of the letters attributed to Paul also mention coauthors. As a result, Botha imagines a more complex situation of authorship and delivery for Paul's letters. "We must become aware of a much more complex event: some persons combined their efforts to deliberate and 'perform' a letter; there was someone involved in the creation and transportation of it, finally 'recreating' for others a presentation/performance of the 'message' intended for sharing" (22). In actual fact, we should imagine not one (singular) "more complex event." The three distinct moments of composition, transportation, and performance represent three different "more complex events." Before he turns to Galatians itself, Botha offers brief discussions of all three of these events (1992:22–7; see also 1993b:415–19).

At about the same time that Botha turned his attention to the thoroughly oral and embodied context of the composition, transmission, and performance of Paul's letters, he also surveys the widespread "reserve towards writing in the Graeco-Roman world" (1993a). He begins with the invention of the Phoenician alphabet and its importation to Greece and quickly chronicles the rise of literacy among Greek and Roman cultures. In the context of this rising literacy, "the evidence indicates a society that is still largely oral with quite distinct (in comparison to modern notions) attitudes towards literacy. Hellenistic culture flourished at the same time that a complex relationship developed between oral and written modes of thought and communication" (745). In this "complex relationship," both reading and writing were technical—even vocational—skill sets that were not necessarily linked to power, education, or wealth. So one Pompeian businessman has at least one dealing involving 100,000 sesterces interest a month, but this businessman is illiterate and unable to write a simple business receipt (see 747). Two and a half centuries later, a lector (!) in an Egyptian village church uses a scribe to certify an affidavit because he "does not know letters" (see 748)![25] This complex relationship between orality and writing moves Botha to turn to passages from Papias and Clement of Alexandria and postulate "tensions within early Christianity" (756) between oral and written communicative media.

In his more recent publications, Pieter Botha has turned his attention more narrowly to the practices of reading (2005) and writing (2009a) written texts, as well as the written texts themselves (2009b), in concrete cultural perspective. As we have seen, these issues arose already in Botha's earlier work, especially his essays on Paul (1992; 1993b). With respect to reading, Botha draws our attention to differences between our relationship, as readers, to the written NT texts from the first-century CE Christians' relationship, as readers and audiences, to those same texts. "Even if their texts have come down to us unchanged . . . our relation to those texts cannot be the same as that of readers in the past *because* reading has a history" (2005:622). Botha makes exactly the same point about authorship: "[W]e need to understand that 'authorship' has a history. . . . Whereas authorship was, in earlier times, intimately part of patronage it has become, for us, something determined by printing, literary property, censorship and income" (2009a:496). Across two decades of publishing, Botha has consistently attempted to place early Christian texts, including the circumstances of their authorship and their reading, into historical perspective.

Kenneth E. Bailey

In 1991, around the same time that Joanna Dewey, Paul Achtemeier, and Pieter Botha were beginning to issue NT media-critical scholarship, Kenneth Bailey published his essay, "Informal Controlled Oral Tradition and the Synoptic Gospels," a relatively short article in a relatively obscure journal, the *Asia Journal of Theology*. (The journal *Themelios* reprinted Bailey's essay four years later and made it more broadly accessible to European and American audiences; see also Bailey 1995b.) Bailey spent over three decades living in the Middle East, and he sets out to offer a model of the transmission of oral tradition on the basis of his experiences living in the same region as Jesus (albeit, nearly two millennia later).[26] "Our own experience has uncovered a specific discernible methodology functioning in traditional Middle Eastern village" (1995a:4).

Bailey begins by contrasting his model of "informal controlled tradition" with two alternatives. First, he describes Bultmann's form-critical model of the transmission of oral tradition, which Bailey calls an "informal uncontrolled." That is, the tradition is "informal" in the sense there are no clearly defined teachers, students, or social and communicative structures to facilitate the transmission of the tradition. It is "uncontrolled" in the sense that the tradition "is open to new additions and new shapes" (1995a:5). The early Christians had no interest in preserving Jesus' teaching and accounts of his life, but as they created new teachings and accounts they readily and regularly attributed those new "traditions" to Jesus. Bailey acknowledges informal uncontrolled tradition in the Middle East today, but he likens this to "rumour transmission" (5).

Second, Bailey describes Gerhardsson's comparative model of the transmission of the Jesus tradition, which he calls "formal controlled." That is, the tradition is "formal" in the sense that the roles of teacher and student are clearly defined, and the processes by which the teaching is expressed and transmitted are tightly structured. It is "controlled" in the sense that the tradition is memorized, fixed, and preserved intact apart from the teachings of other doctrinal authorities (5). Again, Bailey acknowledges formal controlled tradition in the Middle East today, such as in the modern memorization of the Qur'an (5).

Against both Bultmann and Gerhardsson, Bailey proposes an "informal controlled" model of oral tradition on the basis of his anecdotal experience in the Middle East, which in Bailey's estimation "has all the markings of an ancient methodology" (6). Bailey refers to the cultural tradition of the *haflat samar*, evening gatherings in which a "community is *preserving* its store of tradition" (6; italics in the original). These gatherings are "informal" in the sense that they do not involve a clearly defined teacher (or speaker) or students (or hearers). However, the community (especially the elders) exercise a measure of control over the tradition expressed. Despite the flexibility permitted for the expression of tradition, the community will intervene if the essential elements of the tradition are altered, omitted, or falsified. According to Bailey, the *haflat samar* would include the following kinds of material: proverbs, story riddles, poetry, parables, and historical accounts of important local figures (6–7). Bailey then proceeds to discuss the three levels of control the community might exercise over their traditions: no flexibility (for proverbs and poems), some flexibility (for parables and historical accounts), and total flexibility (7–8).[27]

Bailey's model of informal controlled oral tradition, like Gerhardsson's model of rabbinic instruction, is built on concrete data regarding a community's oral communications. This is the first and perhaps primary strength of his model.[28] Moreover, Bailey's model draws attention to the specific social mechanisms ("controls") that enable the oral expression of tradition to remain stable across multiple performances *as well as* to vary in periphery details, style, or moral lesson. Unfortunately, Bailey uses the word "authenticity" to refer to the stability of informal controlled oral tradition.[29] "Authenticity," especially among historians of Jesus, does not mean "stability" but "actuality." When a historian of Jesus describes the account of Jesus' baptism in the Jordan by John as "authentic," she means that Jesus was actually baptized, not that the accounts of Jesus' baptism remained stable in the decades following the event. Understandably, then, Theodore Weeden has fundamentally misread Bailey's essay when he refers to "the authentic, uncorrupted historical core of a community's oral tradition," and "preserving uncorrupted the archaic, original historical facts" (Weeden 2009:33; see also 35–7). Perhaps Weeden should be forgiven for misreading Bailey's unfortunate word, but the fact remains that Weeden has fundamentally misread Bailey's article at this very crucial juncture.

Bailey's anecdotal approach to modeling the oral Jesus tradition has made an impressive impact on NT scholarship, especially when we keep in mind that, to use James Dunn's remarkable understatement, Bailey's work "appeared in not so prominent journals" (Dunn 2009:44). Specifically, N. T. Wright and James D. G. Dunn, two behemoths of NT and historical Jesus scholarship, have found Bailey's model useful for understanding something of the pre-Gospel oral Jesus tradition as well as for explaining the similarities and differences of the Gospels' stories about Jesus.[30] I would even go so far as to say that, thanks to Wright and especially

Dunn, the *impact* of Bailey's work on NT scholarship in general rivals Kelber's (though Bailey's work in no way compares to Kelber's in terms of its volume or its sophistication).[31]

Richard Horsley

We have already begun to see that interest in biblical media criticism was picking up steam in the mid-1990s. Richard Horsley began to pay attention to issues of media as part of his developing interest in the ascendance of an explicitly literary criticism of NT texts (see Horsley 1994:1, 135).[32] Horsley's full-blown interest in media criticism would become manifest at the turn of the millennium with the publication of two studies, one focused on Q (Horsley, with Draper 1999) and the other on Mark (2001). Like Dewey (whose work we introduced above), Horsley focuses his attention on the intersection of media criticism and the social distribution of power (e.g. Horsley, with Draper 1999:128–32). He relies heavily on the sociology of conflict and the anthropology of marginal and/ or oppressed cultures (esp. the work of James C. Scott), and so his conception of power and the exercise of power is not as simplistic or imprecise as Dewey's.

Horsley's media theory is more influenced by John Miles Foley than by Walter Ong and Eric Havelock.[33] As a result, Horsley avoids spending too much energy on the *composition* of the NT texts (see Kelber 1983; Dewey 1989, 1991, 2008) and focuses instead on the *function* of written NT texts—including Q—within their specific sociocultural environments (Horsley, with Draper 1999:132–49; Horsley 2001:61–78). Horsley argues, on the basis of the cost and complexity of ancient scrolls, "One may doubt that many Judean or Galilean village assemblies (*synagogai* [*sic*]) in late second-temple times owned Torah scrolls . . . scrolls were costly, and it seems doubtful that very many village assemblies could have afforded them" (1999:136, 137). Despite acknowledging that some Jewish communities clearly had biblical scrolls available to them, Horsley underestimates the presence of written texts even in the more rural villages of Galilee and Judea. Even in the absence of written texts, people often behaved as though texts were present. For example, in his account of Jesus teaching in the Temple during the Feast of Tabernacles, John nowhere portrays Jesus as actually reading from a written scroll. Nevertheless, "the Jews" respond to Jesus' teaching with amazement that he, apparently, "knows letters" (i.e. he has read and studied the biblical texts) despite his evidently apparent lack of education (Jn 7.15).[34] Horsley's analyses ought to take greater account of the potential for the social function and cultural currency not just of written *tradition* but of actual written *texts* to "render the actual presence of a text superfluous" (Stock 1983:7).

*   *   *

We have only just begun to survey some of the more influential voices in NT media-critical research; unfortunately, we have left out more than we have included.[35] To compound the problem, our choices to include some scholars but leave out others have resulted in a narrow presentation of the wider field of NT media criticism. For example, if we had surveyed the works of Antoinette Wire or Holly Hearon, we would have focused more attention on storytelling and the light that such studies have shed on the NT. Or again, if we had highlighted Tom Boomershine or David Rhoads, we would have focused more attention on performance criticism and the effects that actually performing NT texts has on interpreting, understanding, and applying the texts in modern contexts. (Joanna Dewey is also an important performance-critical voice.) And so on. We have made some significant decisions in this chapter, and those decisions have consequences.

Even so, hopefully the material I have included suffices to achieve the purpose of the present chapter: to provide a basic introduction to the history of discussion of oral tradition and the NT and to some of the more commonly cited voices in that discussion. This and the previous chapter have provided a basic introduction to the field of NT media criticism. The next two chapters, which together comprise Part Two of this book, demonstrate what NT media criticism looks like. In the next chapter, we will consider two common approaches to the question of oral tradition and the NT. We can describe these two approaches in the broadest of strokes. The first, which I will call the *morphological approach* to oral tradition and the NT, attempts to find the remnants, the traces, the residue of oral tradition in written texts. The second, which I will call the *contextual approach* to oral tradition and the NT, identifies oral tradition as the context within which oral-derived (written) texts become meaningful vehicles of communication. These two approaches are not diametrically opposed to one another, though I will argue that only one of them holds any potential for enhancing our interpretations of the written NT texts.

PART TWO

A demonstration of biblical media criticism

CHAPTER FOUR

The *how* of oral tradition and NT studies

We have already caught a glimpse of two broad approaches to the question of oral tradition and the NT, though unfortunately many have not noticed (or at least have not commented upon) the differences between them. The most visible approach, which we have already encountered in Kelber's early work (1983) and in Dewey's and Botha's analyses, among others, postulates certain identifiable features of orality. Once a researcher finds such features in a particular text, s/he assumes these to be residual traces of prewritten oral tradition. The second approach rejects (or at least does not emphasize) the idea that orality has certain stylistic or morphological effects upon a tradition and approaches written texts as completely textual artifacts (or phenomena). In this second approach, oral tradition highlights the question of *how* our textual artifacts were composed, performed, received, and transmitted within specific cultural contexts and/or concrete social settings. This chapter briefly surveys and evaluates both approaches and, in the final analysis, advocates for the second while problematizing the first.

The morphological approach to oral tradition and the NT

Morphology refers, among other things, to the form, shape, or structure of a thing. I refer to the first approach to oral tradition and the NT as the "morphological approach" because scholars of this persuasion look for orality's *shape* (or its *form*) in written texts. This approach to oral tradition is not unique to biblical scholars.

Albert Lord's seminal book, *The Singer of Tales* (1960), launched an entire academic discipline as researchers began looking for the visible effects—the morphological telltale signs—of orality on traditional texts from around the world and throughout history. According to Lord, the analysis of formulaic language can

> indicate whether any given text is oral or "literary." An *oral* text will yield a predominance of clearly demonstrable formulas, with the bulk of the remainder "formulaic," and a small number of nonformulaic expressions. A *literary* text will show a predominance of nonformulaic expressions, with some formulaic expressions, and very few clear formulas. (1960:130; italics in the original)

Lord uses "formula" in a very specific, technical sense, as "a group of words which is regularly employed under the same metrical conditions to express a given essential idea" (30). Lord also expands the concept of the formula to include certain type-scenes, or themes, such as a council meeting or the gathering of an army. "The theme, even though it be verbal, is not any fixed set of words, but a grouping of ideas" (69). That is, a grouping of ideas becomes traditional, or formulaic, and includes a regular and predictable set of characteristics, even though the words that express those ideas can vary between performances.

The application of Oral-Formulaic Theory to the NT texts, especially the Gospels, has come under some criticism for generic reasons: namely, the NT texts are not poetry, metric or otherwise (e.g. Hurtado 1997).[1] The Slavic poetry that Albert Lord and his teacher, Milman Parry, recorded and analyzed was a metrical phenomenon that featured ten-syllable lines. Similarly, the Homeric poetry in the *Iliad* and the *Odyssey*, which Parry and Lord also analyzed, is metric poetry. The Gospels and Acts, by way of contrast, are prose narratives, Paul's letters (and the General Epistles, in varying measure), of course, are epistolary. As a result, the formulaic language of Slavic or Homeric epic differs substantially from the language of the NT.

But the formulaic language of oral traditional epic was only one aspect of Lord's theory; he devoted nearly just as much space to the function of the *theme* in the composition-in-performance of oral traditional epic (see Lord 1960:68–98). Lord defines *theme* as "the groups of ideas regularly used in telling a tale in the formulaic style of traditional song" (68). The form critics similarly identified a "formulaic style" in the Gospels. That is, they noticed that the Gospels were made up of a limited number of story types. The form critics therefore set out to produce a comprehensive list of forms (= themes) within the Gospels, among other things.[2] They also assumed that these forms developed through time according to certain evolutionary laws of oral transmission (e.g. that stories tended to get longer, become more detailed or less Semitic, etc.).[3] The form-critical assumption that oral forms follow certain evolutionary laws has a counterpart in orality studies, in which oral cultures are said to exhibit certain general tendencies or characteristics.

Very often, NT media critics refer to the characteristics, norms, or patterns of orality without clearly stating which features of oral expression they have in mind. When they do identify specific features, they typically turn to Walter Ong's list of nine "characteristics of orally based thought and expression" (1982:36–56).[4] Ong described these characteristics as patterns that "set off orally based thought and expression from chirographically and typographically based thought and expression, the characteristics, that is, which are most likely to strike those reared in writing and print cultures as surprising" (1983:36). Before we present Ong's list, we need to point out explicitly that he is not attempting to describe the distinctive features of oral *communication* but is rather positing a more abstract phenomenon: oral *thought*.[5] We should be aware that, when adherents to the morphological approach speak of "oral tradition," they have often (if not usually) switched the referent of the key adjective, *oral*, and are no longer interested in tradition orally *expressed* but rather are focused on tradition orally *conceived*. Someone might ask, "But what is 'orally conceived tradition'?" Ong's list of nine psychodynamics of orality provides the primary answer to that question. Ong introduces his list as follows: "In a primary oral culture, thought and expression tend to be of the following sorts" (1982:37):

1 *Additive rather than subordinative* (Ong 1982:37–8)
  Rather than define this characteristic, Ong merely points to the example of Gen. 1.1–5, which uses the Hebrew conjunction *w-* ("and") nine times. Essentially, Ong is referring to parataxis, which we defined in Chapter Two as "placing simple sentences alongside one another by means of a coordinating conjunction (and, but, for, etc.) rather than a subordinating conjunction (after, since, in order that, etc.)." Young provides a more helpful definition than does Ong: "In place of the complex logical constructions with subordinate clauses that one finds in written compositions, in oral-derived texts one will tend to find phrases strung together and linked by additive or purposive connectives (e.g., 'and then,' 'and next' or 'for')" (2011:84).

2 *Aggregative rather than analytic* (Ong 1982:38–9) "The elements of orally based thought and expression tend to be not so much simple integers as clusters of integers, such as parallel terms or phrases or clauses, antithetical terms or phrases or clauses, epithets" (Ong 1982:38). Ong is referring here to the formulaic quality of tradition composed-in-performance that Milman Parry and Albert Lord championed. "Oral expression thus carries a load of epithets and other formulary baggage which high literacy rejects as cumbersome and tiresomely redundant because of its aggregative weight" (38).

3 *Redundant or "copious"* (Ong 1982:39–41) Ong's third psychodynamic is the first one for which he actually offers a causal relationship with an oral medium. Whereas written texts allow the reader to "backloop" or remind himself of what he has already read, oral discourse does not persist long enough for hearers to remind themselves of what they heard without the risk of missing what they are presently hearing. "There is nothing to backloop into outside the

mind, for the oral utterance has vanished as soon as it is uttered. Hence the mind must move ahead more slowly . . . Redundancy, repetition of the just-said, keeps both speaker and hearer surely on the track" (Ong 1982:39–40). Young extends Ong's concept of redundancy by augmenting it with Immanent Art, Foley's approach to oral and oral-derived works of verbal art: "oft-repeated formulas or patterns may function as a shorthand referent to complex ideas that are transparent to one familiar with the tradition being performed, a 'traditional referentiality' that 'enables an extremely economical transaction of meaning'" (Young 2011:85, citing Foley 1999:11).

4 *Conservative or traditionalist* (Ong 1982:41–2) This fourth characteristic arises fairly directly from the preceding one: "Since in a primary oral culture conceptualized knowledge that is not repeated aloud soon vanishes, oral societies must invest great energy in saying over and over again what has been learned arduously over the ages. This need establishes a highly traditionalist or conservative set of mind that with good reason inhibits intellectual experimentation" (1982:41). Ong acknowledges that literate thought can also be conservative rather than innovative, and that "oral cultures do not lack originality of their own kind" (41). Thus it seems to me that Ong has not merely given with one hand and taken with the other; his qualifications and caveats of this fourth psychodynamic give with one hand and take with both!

5 *Close to the human lifeworld* (Ong 1982:42–3) Oral expressions and thought structure knowledge concretely and express that knowledge in terms of actions and events rather than abstractly and without context. "Knowledge in an oral context is conceptualized and communicated in a manner that remains closely related to the familiar, everyday world of human activity" (Young 2011:88).

6 *Agonistically toned* (Ong 1982:43–5) Since oral cultures structure and communicate knowledge "close to the human lifeworld," they also associate pieces of knowledge (or data) with people. Whereas a literate culture "separates the

knower from the known," oral culture situates knowledge within the context of struggle, conflict, debate, and verbal (or literal) combat. Conversely, "[t]he other side of name-calling or vituperation in oral or residually oral cultures is the fulsome expression of praise which is found everywhere in connection with orality" (1982:45). Oral thought is capable of condemning as well as praising; it does not, as a rule, offer neutral descriptions.

7 *Empathetic and participatory rather than objectively distanced* (Ong 1982:45–6) If we accept that orally conceived knowledge is both "close to the human lifeworld" and "agonistically toned," learning and internalizing knowledge involves identifying with the person or people associated with that knowledge. Oral thought does not exhibit the distance, the objectivity, afforded by literate thought. As a result, learners and hearers (i.e. audiences) identify with the content of an oral tradition and experience a communal, collective response to that tradition.

8 *Homeostatic* (Ong 1982:46–9) This psychodynamic is the flip-side of nos. 3 and 4, above ("redundant or 'copious'"; "conservative or traditionalist"). Repetition preserves knowledge, conserving it in the present for the future. Orality does not have any mechanisms for preserving knowledge apart from repetition. As a result, an oral culture regularly repeats knowledge that bears some relevance for current needs, but knowledge that bears little or no relevance for the present is not repeated and eventually is forgotten.[6]

9 *Situational rather than abstract* (Ong 1982:49–57) This ninth psychodynamic is very similar to the fifth ("close to the human lifeworld"): "Oral cultures tend to use concepts in situational, operational frames of reference that are minimally abstract in the sense that they remain close to the living human lifeworld" (1982:49).

Ong himself offered this list as a way of suggesting the general distinctiveness of primary orality *vis-à-vis* literacy, which distinctiveness allegedly fades during the twilight of residual orality. "This inventory of characteristics is not presented as exclusive or conclusive but as suggestive" (1983:36). Young adds two other characteristics of orality to Ong's list: "both variable and stable" (2011:87),[7] and "mnemonically constructed" (89–91).[8] Though we may expect to find some variation in the details, when media critics (of the NT or otherwise) speak of the traits, characteristics, or norms of oral thought and expression, they invariably refer to Ong's list of nine psychodynamics. I have some doubts that orality—whether orally expressed tradition or oral patterns of thought—is necessarily or universally all of these things. More importantly, however, these characteristics are not distinctively *oral* features of communication or thought; we can find any and all of them in literate communication as well.[9] If these are not essentially and exclusively *oral* characteristics, then it seems to me that they lose all utility for identifying the shape or form of oral tradition in written texts.

New Testament media critics have largely accepted the idea that oral cultures exhibit particular cultural or cognitive characteristics, and that these characteristics (or psychodynamics) differ from literate cultural and cognitive psychodynamics. This acceptance is understandable. This idea results in a fairly straightforward research agenda: to identify distinctively oral psychodynamics—cultural as well as cognitive—and look for those characteristics in written texts. Perhaps the most industrious and focused NT scholar pursuing this research agenda is Joanna Dewey. She has explicitly set out to identify characteristics of orality in Mark's Gospel and to use those characteristics to explain how Mark was written and organized. As we saw in the previous chapter, her research depends on the orality of certain literary features, such as chiasms ("ring structures"), repetition, parataxis, and others. If, however, these features are not necessarily and essentially oral, then conclusions based on their alleged orality begin to unravel.[10]

So I find it especially interesting that Dewey's published doctoral thesis, *Markan Public Debate*, portrayed many of these features as *literary* (= written, not oral) techniques. Dewey identifies six literary techniques, as well as five additional rhetorical techniques, that characterize Mark's Gospel (1980:31–4). These techniques include the use of hook words, repetition, and chiasms and ring structures. Dewey was already aware that "many if not all of [these literary techniques] have their origin in oral literatures" (29), and she even describes inclusio as "a recognized technique of oral literatures" (31).[11] Nevertheless, she persists in describing all these narrative features as "techniques which can be used in written composition," and she even denies any "clear difference between oral and written composition for popular literature in the first century C.E." (29). Her extensive references to Charles Talbert's book, *Literary Patterns, Theological Themes and the Genre of Luke-Acts* (1974), reinforces the impression that, early in her career, Dewey was convinced of the literary origins of the Gospel of Mark, and this *on the basis of the very same features that she later identifies as evidence that Mark is an oral narrative*!

Nine years later, when she published her first media-critical essay on Mark (1989), she changed her description of certain narrative characteristics without offering an explanation why. For example, we can compare Dewey's earlier and later descriptions of inclusio (the repetition of an idea at the beginning and end of a literary unit that establishes that unit as a coherent entity; see Table 4.1).

TABLE 4.1 Joanna Dewey's definitions of inclusio

Markan Public Debate (1980)	"Oral Methods" (1989)
Inclusio. The repetition of the same word or phrase at or near the beginning and ending of some unit, a sentence, a pericope, or a larger section. The form of the word need not be repeated exactly. For instance, one might find a noun and a verb from the same root. Inclusio is by definition an indication of structure, the beginning and end of a rhetorical unit of any size. It is a recognized technique of oral literatures. So the rhetorical critic by designating certain repetitions as inclusios is making a judgment about the limits of some unit of narrative (Dewey 1980:31).	Oral narrative "operates on the acoustic principle of the echo." Ring composition (inclusio) is endemic in oral narrative, marking the boundaries of individual episodes and of much longer sections. Ong notes that individual episodes and clusters of episodes are narrated in balanced patterns in either parallel or chiastic order. Havelock comments that when we notice these correspondences at all, we tend to call them "patterns," a visual concept; rather, he says, we should think of them as acoustic responses (Dewey 1989:38–9, citing Ong 1982; Havelock 1984).

As I said above, in 1980 Dewey emphasized the "literary-ness" of the inclusio as a feature of Mark's written narrative.[12] Her nod to the inclusio as "a recognized technique of oral literatures" (31) only reinforces her blurring of the distinction between oral and written composition just two pages earlier (29–30). In 1980 Dewey gave no indication whatsoever that she thought of inclusio as an overtly oral technique of composition.

Nearly a decade later, when she described inclusio as "endemic in oral narrative" (1989:38) and referred to "typical *oral* techniques" (40; emphasis added), we might expect some explanation for such a significant change of view. We find none. Instead, we find only that she has read Eric Havelock (and Walter Ong). The only justification she offers for describing specific narrative techniques as necessarily "oral" is a comparison between Mark and "the structural characteristics of oral narrative, as described primarily by Havelock, the foremost student of the shift from oral to written media in Greek culture" (34). If she can find in the Gospel of Mark the supposedly oral psychodynamics that Havelock identifies in Plato, then her case is made that "oral compositional means pervade the larger Gospel narrative" (34). But readers should notice that she never even raises the question why these narrative features are necessarily *oral*!

We see the problem immediately when we get to Dewey's presentation of Havelock's research. "Plato considers the content of mimesis to be merely *doxa* or opinion, which has three limitations: It is made up of happenings (*gignomena*), not abstract thought; the happenings are visually concrete (*horata*); and they are many (*polla*), that is, pluralized, not organized according to cause and effect" (34, citing Havelock 1963:180). Any narrative that (1) consists of happenings, (2) which are visually concrete, and (3) which are not organized according to cause and effect must be an oral narrative. Moreover, the preservation of these three features in written narratives indicates that the narrative in question was originally developed in an oral mode.

A significant problem undermines Dewey's line of reasoning. If the features that she (and Havelock) have identified as the result of oral psychodynamics continue to function properly in written narratives—as clearly they do—then we will need some explanation as to why repetitions, or ring structures, or parataxis, and so on are evidence of oral narratives *and not of written narratives*.[13] The very fact that these features work perfectly well in oral narratives as well as in written narratives reveals the absurdity of calling them *oral* features in any restrictive sense. The features themselves are neither necessarily oral nor necessarily written. They are features of both oral and written narratives.

A potentially more fruitful example of the morphological approach to questions of oral tradition in our written texts—especially in the Gospels—focuses on the observable patterns of variability and stability in the texts. We can see this approach to oral tradition especially in the works of James Dunn and his recent student, Terence Mournet. For example, as early as 2002 Dunn provided a list of "five characteristic features of oral transmission of tradition that deserve attention" (93).[14] I want to focus on Dunn's last characteristic feature. "Fifth and finally, oral tradition is characteristically (I do not say distinctively) a combination of *fixity* and *flexibility*, of *stability* and *diversity*" (2005:98; italics in the original). Dunn would later explain that these very features in the synoptic tradition, which tells largely the same story of Jesus but with frequent differences in detail, sparked his interest in Kenneth Bailey's anecdotal description of oral tradition.

> As one who had always been fascinated by the character of the Synoptic tradition—teaching substantially the same but diverse in detail and grouping, narratives evidently of the same events yet often very different in introduction, length, particular wording and conclusion—I found that [Bailey's] anecdotes . . . provided a plausible explanation which I had never heard or considered earlier. This, I should perhaps emphasize, is what most attracted me to [Bailey's] thesis: that it *provided such a good explanation of the character of the Synoptic tradition*, a character which is so clearly evident in the Synoptic tradition as we still have it—the same yet different, firm in substance yet variant in detail. (Dunn 2009:45; italics in the original)

In other words, the fact of the striking interplay of similarity and difference between the Gospels, especially Matthew, Mark, and Luke, resonates with Bailey's description of informal controlled oral tradition. The written Gospels, therefore, must be the results of oral traditional processes like those Bailey set forth. As N. T. Wright stated in very strong terms, "Until it is shown that the process Bailey envisages is historically impossible, I propose that it be taken as a working model" (1996:136).

Similarly, Dunn's student Terrence Mournet objects to using literary terminology ("text," "literature," etc.) to discuss oral phenomena. "[D]escribing an oral performance as a 'text' can conjure up images of fixity and stability often associated with a fixed manuscript tradition, when in fact the vast majority of oral performances are more flexible than fixed" (2005:16).[15] When he turns his attention to the "characteristics of oral tradition" (174–90) and specifically to "variability: flexibility and stability of oral tradition" (179–90), Mournet helpfully quotes Albert Lord: "One of the earmarks of an oral traditional narrative is its textual fluidity, which is to say, because it has no fixed original it is constantly being repeated without concern for word-for-word retelling of a set, established text" (Lord 1978:37, cited by Mournet 2005:180). Anyone who has spent even five minutes with a Gospel synopsis would have no trouble applying this description of "oral traditional narrative" to the Gospels of Matthew, Mark, and Luke. But oral tradition is not only variable and flexible, and Mournet is careful to pay attention also to the mechanisms that enable oral tradition to exhibit considerable stability (2005:184–7). Bailey's discussion of oral traditions that experience "some flexibility" (see Bailey 1995a:7–8) coheres well with Lord's discussion of "songs and the song" (see Lord 1960:99–123). As a result, Mournet identifies the "synthesis" of variability and stability as one of the most significant advances offered to NT scholarship from the field of folkloristics (a quintessentially oral discipline; see Mournet 2005:189–90).

Both Dunn and Mournet have provided excellent (and sorely needed!) discussions of the qualities one finds in the synoptic tradition. I have no desire to dispute anything they have said, except for this one point: Neither the variability, nor the stability, nor the synthesis of variability and stability that Dunn and Mournet discuss are necessarily and essentially oral characteristics. The prominent British textual critic David Parker focused on the *written* manuscript tradition of the Gospels in his famous little book, *The Living Text of the Gospels* (1997). When he mentions "the inevitably provisional character of all manuscript copies" (204), Parker is referring to the irreducible variability of chirographic texts, which are *performed* in the act of copying and so are subject to all the processes of emendation, alteration, abbreviation, and expansion that characterize oral tradition. But even as forces of variability and fluidity affect the transmission of manuscripts, contrary forces of stability and fixity also come into play. For example, even the "particularly dramatic" differences between the texts of Lk. 6.1–10 in the codices Vaticanus (B/02), Bezae (D/05), and Dionysiou (Ω/045) do not obscure the fact that these very different readings are all variants of the same literary unit from the Gospels.[16] Even the American textual critic Bart Ehrman concedes the essential stability of the NT manuscript tradition.[17]

In light of the simultaneous stability and variability of the NT manuscript tradition, brought into crisp focus by both Parker and Ehrman, I cannot follow Dunn and Mournet in attributing stability and variability to oral media. Dunn and Mournet are both aware that oral tradition is not fixed-but-flexible *in contrast to* written tradition (see Dunn 2005:98; Mournet 2005:100–1, n. 2). But for some reason, both Dunn and Mournet persist in describing stability and variability—and especially the interplay between the two—as "characteristics of oral tradition." Though they have given helpful and insightful descriptions of the dynamics of fluidity and fixity in the synoptic tradition, those dynamics belong to the tradition itself and are not the effects of the tradition's medium.

New Testament media critics have not spent all their attention on the Gospel narratives. Media critics have also applied the morphological approach to oral tradition and the NT to Paul's letters. Casey Davis, for example, has suggested that certain words, phrases, and forms in Philippians are oral formulas or themes (1999:90–6). As examples, he mentions the couplet *amemptos* and *amōmos* ("pure" and "without blemish") in Phil. 2.15. He describes phrases such as *en Christō* ("in Christ") and *dikaiosynē theou* ("righteousness of God") as particularly formulaic aspects of Paul's language. Even more problematically, Davis addresses certain epistolary elements under the heading "Oral Themes" (Davis 1999:95–6). For example, he discusses the distinctive Pauline greeting, "Grace to you, and peace from God our Father and the Lord Jesus Christ" (Phil. 1.2), the thanksgiving formula (1.3), and the confidence formula (1.6), among others, as possible "oral themes." We can agree with Davis that these epistolary elements enable Paul's letter to function as an oral act of communication, especially inasmuch as they establish the relational connection between Paul, as sender, and the Philippian congregations, as recipients. However, these are distinctly *literary* forms, elements that enable the oral function of Paul's (written) *letter*. Davis has fundamentally misrepresented them by casting them as "oral themes." They are no more "oral" than any other element of Paul's letter to the Philippians, which Paul certainly expected and intended to be read publicly before gathered congregation(s).

Studies that adopt the morphological approach to oral tradition and the NT raise the question, How can scholars refer to written phenomena as oral in any meaningful sense? While nearly every media critic is aware of this question, a surprising number of them never actually address it. Stephen Young is not one of these. Young offers a helpful discussion that provides a careful, but ultimately unsuccessful, presentation of the morphological approach. Walter Ong's list of nine "psychodynamics of orality" play a significant role here, and Young reproduces Ong's list with only minor variations.[18] But before he turns to Ong's list, Young turns to the work of Homerist Egbert Bakker to explain why he treats certain features of written texts as distinctively oral phenomena. In his book, *Pointing at the Past*,[19] Bakker uses the word *oral* to refer to "the *conception* that underlies a discourse" (2005:39; emphasis in the original). He explicitly distinguishes this "conceptual" sense of *oral* from its normal sense as "a medium of communication."

When Bakker explains the difference between discourse that is orally conceived versus that which is conceived as "literate," he can only explain the distinction in vague and unexplained abstractions. According to Bakker,

> As a medium, "oral" excludes "written" in the sense that at the moment of its reception a discourse usually cannot, for us, be both spoken and written at the same time: it has to be either phonic or graphic. In the dimension of conception, on the other hand, the relation between "oral" and its opposite is quite different. "Oral" and "literate" can here be seen as the two poles or extremes of a continuum, with numerous gradations in between. On the one extreme, a discourse is maximally "oral," making full, and necessary, use of the requirements of the spoken medium; on the other extreme a discourse is maximally literate, written exclusively according to the requirements of the written medium in the culture at hand. In practice, most discourses will

display both oral and literate features in varying ratios, being situated at some point between the two extremes. (39)

A number of obvious questions go unanswered (and even unasked). For example, what "requirements," specifically, does Bakker think accompany "the spoken medium"? Second, and conversely, what "requirements" accompany "the written medium"? Third, if we take seriously Bakker's caveat, "in the culture at hand," then how do we quantify the extent to which a given discourse's specific features are the result of its "medium of conception," on the one hand, and to what extent those features result from other cultural factors? And fourth, if a discourse can be wholly "written" in terms of its medium but "oral" in terms of its conception, why should we apply media terminology ("oral," or "literate") to the features of their discourse in the first place?

Bakker goes on to depict the distinction between and interconnection of oral and written media, on the one hand, and oral and literate discourse, on the other, as three related continua, as shown in Table 4.2.

He argues that, as the conception of a discourse moves from left to right along the continuum of oral-to-literate, the dynamics of its writing shift from transcription (writing that *follows* composition) to composition (writing as the *act* of composition). Similarly, the dynamics of reading an orally conceived discourse requires the human voice as it "retranscodes signs seen into sounds heard: the reader's voice turns sight into sound, and in doing so is just as physical as the writer's hand" (Bakker 2005:40). At the literate end of the spectrum, the reading voice becomes metaphorical as neither the author, the text, nor the reader requires the spoken word to communicate the intended message.

TABLE 4.2 The conception of language, writing, and reading

conception of a discourse:	oral <—> literate
conception of its writing:	transcription <—> composition
conception of its reading:	human voice <—> silent reading

Source: Bakker 2005:40[20]

The movement between transcription and composition, and the recognition of shades of difference between them, is helpful, especially when we turn to consider the relationship between an oral-derived text and its larger traditional context. Similarly, the movement between reading aloud ("human voice") and silent reading is also helpful, especially when we turn to consider the dynamics in which an oral-derived text was performed before an audience. However, the first continuum points at nothing, since written language is not essentially and necessarily subordinative, analytic, innovative, or any other thing.[21] Instead, written language can be just as additive, aggregative, and traditionalist as oral language.[22] If not, media critics would not be able to find such language in written texts, and the morphological approach to oral tradition in written texts would have nothing to look for. The question whether oral language can be just as subordinative, analytic, and/ or innovative as written language is somewhat more controversial than its converse. But these questions hardly matter here. If written language can naturally and organically exhibit the features media critics ascribe to oral language, then the basis for ascribing them to orality vanishes. And if these features are not products of orality, then all justification for referring to them as distinctively and peculiarly "oral phenomena" (or as "the psychodynamics of orality") vanishes.[23] In other words, Bakker's second sense of "oral"—as "the *conception* that underlies a discourse" (2005:39)— does not actually describe a difference between oral and written (or "literate") patterns of thought and speech.

Therefore, Stephen Young's use of Bakker's work builds a foundation on unstable grounds. In his explanation of Bakker's distinction between oral and literate conceptions of language, Young refers to "norms that govern spoken interaction [and] norms that govern literate communication" (2011:71). But, speaking frankly, these "norms" do not exist. When Young presents a list of these norms, which largely reproduces Ong's nine psychodynamics of orality (see Ong 1982:36–57), we find the same problem that we find with every appeal to Ong's list: Written communication is just as capable of being of being additive, aggregative, conservative, and so on as oral communication. In fact, biblical scholars (including Young) appeal to Ong's list *in order to explain features of written texts*.[24] But we find an additional problem: Bakker's influence over Young's theoretical approach to oral tradition leads Young to misunderstand "oral-derived text," one of the most important concepts to be taken into account for ancient texts' relationship to oral tradition:

> If a discourse was oral in its conception, and is then transcribed, it falls in the category of oral-derived literature. Oral-derived literature will not evince the characteristics usually associated with written discourse simply because spoken phonemes have been replaced with written graphemes.[25] On the contrary, even in its transcribed form, oral-derived discourse will retain certain features that are peculiar to its oral conception, while losing others. (Young 2011:71)

As we will see when we turn to the contextual approach to oral tradition and the NT, when John Miles Foley offers his own four-fold model of oral-derived texts (see Table 4.3), he accounts for three dynamics: composition, performance, and reception. Not once does he mention the "conception of the discourse" or point to allegedly oral characteristics of the work in question. Oral-derived texts are not necessarily composed orally (though they might be), nor are they necessarily transcriptions of an actual oral performance (though again, they might be). Instead, Foley rightly shifts our focus from what an oral-derived text looks like (i.e. what are its structural features) to how an oral-derived text generates meaning.

In the end, I do not think the morphological approach to oral tradition and the NT can work.[26] The morphological approach depends upon two assumptions that, if both true, create too much tension between them. And if either assumption is false, then the whole program falls apart anyway. First, as we have already seen, the morphological approach assumes oral *and not written* psychodynamics produce certain features of linguistic style or certain narrative features. Few media critics address this issue head-on. A few, however, do. For example, David Aune refers to "the central problem bedeviling anyone who claims that oral patterns are present in written texts." He goes on to identify that central problem: "[A]ll of the evidence is contained in written texts" (2009:74). Media-critics of the morphological persuasion attribute these features (repetition, chiasmus, etc.) to the *medium* of communication—to "orality"—rather than the *tradition* being communicated. For all the impressive display of these features in actual oral traditions in the modern world, even if anthropologists could demonstrate that *every* oral tradition is paratactic, visually robust, and repetitious, that would not establish a *causal* connection between the tradition's medium of communication—its "orality"—and the features in question.[27]

Second, the morphological approach assumes that allegedly oral features of tradition survive the transfer from orality to writing. Moreover, media critics interpret their survival as evidence of the tradition's orality. For example, if orality produces narratives that "are many (*polla*), that is, pluralized, not organized according to cause and effect" (Dewey 1989:34), and if Mark's written narrative is *polla*/pluralized, Mark obviously bears the marks of orality even in its current textual (= written) state. Media critics, however, have not produced any evidence that these alleged features of orality are alien, unnatural, or in any other way intrusive to their new medium.[28]

Let us take Mark's parataxis as an example. Mark's incessant use of *kai* ("and") to connect his sentences does indeed strike us as odd, like a preschooler telling a long and rambling narrative. But the oddity (to us) has nothing to do with our unfamiliarity with the oral medium and/or our preference for written texts. After all, the thing that strikes us as odd—Mark's parataxis—is a feature of his *written* narrative. Scholars of orality cannot simply point to parataxis in oral traditions as proof that parataxis in written narratives are relics from those narratives' oral heritage. They need also to demonstrate that parataxis cannot exist in written texts except as an echo of an oral past. As soon as we can admit parataxis as a feature of written narrative, we lose any connection with the prewritten oral narrative that the morphological approach was trying to recover. Mark's parataxis is a feature of his written narrative, and nothing suggests it is an alien survivor from Mark's oral prehistory. In the end, and for these reasons, I do not think the morphological approach to oral tradition and the NT can work.[29]

The contextual approach to oral tradition and the NT

If we cannot find oral tradition *in* the NT, are there other ways that oral traditional research might help us better understand the written texts of the NT? I think it can, and I refer to this "other way" as the contextual approach to oral tradition and the NT. This approach does not look for the shape of oral tradition in the written texts of the NT (see morphological approach, above). Instead, the contextual approach posits the oral expression of tradition as the context within which the written NT texts developed and were written by authors, recited by lectors (and/or oral performers), and received by audiences (and/or readers). A contextual approach to oral tradition and the NT fundamentally changes the questions media critics ask and the issues involved in answering those questions.

How a work becomes meaningful

John Miles Foley arguably has done more than anyone else to explain how oral tradition functions as meaningful social phenomena within specific cultural contexts. Foley explicitly looks past the question of *what* a particular oral tradition means to ask *how* a particular oral tradition becomes meaningful to real people:

> [H]ow do we interpret works of verbal art that either stem directly from or have roots in oral tradition? . . . Instead of looking at oral and oral-derived poems through the interposed lens of literary values and assumptions, . . . we must begin at a much more fundamental level by determining how these poems convey meaning. (Foley 1991:xi, xii)

We can already see that Foley has broadened his focus from simple questions of media (oral vs written) to consider "works of verbal art"—oral performances as well as written texts.[30] This simple change in terminology takes seriously the fact that research into oral tradition often works with non-oral phenomena (musical scores, ethnographic field reports, recordings of oral performances, as well as written texts). All our talk of "orality" too easily obscures the self-evident truism that biblical scholars only ever work with written texts.

Foley's shift of focus to "works of verbal art" has a second useful consequence. It provides another resource to help us escape the gravitational pull of the attractive but outdated theory of the Great Divide, which we have seen continues to lure media critics despite having been widely discredited. The attraction of the Great Divide theory is understandable. Scholars from Rudolf Bultmann to E. P. Sanders have minimized the differences between oral and written communication.[31] Contemporary media critics are laboring to counteract this received wisdom of NT scholarship and demonstrate to other NT scholars that media dynamics affect how we interpret and understand our written texts. But we cannot replace one unhelpful generalization with another. Foley's approach enables us to affirm and to explore the possibility that "forms of verbal art . . . that, although they may survive only as texts, have roots planted firmly in an oral tradition" may have different dynamics than texts without those roots (Foley 1995a:xi).

In order to theorize how oral-traditional works of verbal art communicate meaning to their audiences, Foley identifies two "binary tensions," or "paired tendencies that help to place traditional (both oral and oral-derived) works on a continuum or spectrum of innumerable individual points" (1991:xiv).[32] First, he refers to "the relative balance of *conferred* versus *inherent* meaning. In the modern literary work of art . . . an author (not a tradition) *confers* meaning on his or her creation; if his or her text also draws meaning from literary tradition, it does so only through the careful intercession of the author" (8; italics in the original). In other words, authors of literary texts exert considerable control and influence over the meaning of their texts. They are creative geniuses who marshal words and images and allusions to other texts to convey something new, original, and unprecedented. The authorial "conferred meaning" of overtly literary texts renders those texts creative more than traditional.[33]

Foley contrasts the "conferred meaning" of nontraditional works of verbal art with "traditional works" that marshal words, phrases, and type-scenes (or themes; see above) "that were in place long before the execution of the present version or text, long before the present nominal author learned the inherited craft" (8). The "present nominal author" is not responsible for her words, images, and allusions to other works in the same sense that a nontraditional author is. Therefore, for the traditional author, the meaning of her words, images, and allusions is comparatively independent because that meaning existed before she began to speak or to write. The readers (or audiences) of traditional works are already familiar with the words, phrases, and themes of those works, and so their meaning is conventional, familiar, or "inherent." Every work of verbal art—whether traditional or creative—will evoke both conferred and inherent meanings (rather than one or the other). The difference between traditional works and literary works lies in the balance between these two strategies.

Foley goes on to identify a second binary tension: "Partnered with inherent and conferred meaning, respectively, will be the doublet or tension of 'connotative' and 'denotative' meaning" (xiv). Denotative meaning refers to the strictly textual, "dictionary" level of meaning of words in a given context, whereas connotative meaning refers to the larger traditional associations that attach to words in a given context. Perhaps we can best explain this binary tension with an example. The Greek word *kyrios* means "lord" or "master" and refers, among other things, to persons who hold authority.[34] In light of *kyrios*'s denotative value ("lord" or "master"), Luke's use of *kyrios* in Lk 7.19 is surprising. At the strictly textual, denotative level, nothing in context warrants the epithet *kyrios* in Luke's narrative introduction to John the Baptist's question of Jesus.[35] Jesus has just healed a centurion's sick slave (Lk. 7.1–10) and raised a widow's dead son (7.11–15), and he has been hailed as "a great prophet" (Lk. 7.16). Here in v. 19, then, *kyrios* seems strange.[36] However, given the pervasive use of *kyrios* as a reference to Jesus (see *NIDNTT* 2.514–15), the term came to connote Jesus and could be used in contexts where *kyrios*' connotative value eclipsed its denotative value (such as at Lk. 7.19). In this example, we catch a fleeting glimpse of the untextual (and untextualizable) *tradition* of Jesus-as-Lord (= *kyrios*), the "silent partner" (Foley 1991:xv) that accompanies the Lukan performance of the story of John's question to Jesus. In other words, the larger tradition of Jesus-as-Lord is the *context* within which Luke's anomalous use of *kyrios* in 7.19 makes perfect sense.

How, then, does a text bear its meaning for an author and to a reader when all three entities—(1) text, (2) author/performer, and (3) reader/audience—participate within a larger, contextualizing tradition? Foley argues that a traditional work of verbal art (i.e. one that is not simply the work of a single creative genius) tends to exhibit inherent meaning because it uses traditional words, phrases, and themes already familiar to the audience (and therefore already meaningful for them). Individual performers and/or authors could contribute distinctive nuances and interpretations to the tradition, and some performers were more compelling than others. Even in traditional texts we will have to account for the performer's and/or the author's conferral of meaning.[37] But traditional works exhibit a greater degree of inherent meaning in comparison with increasingly literary or creative works of verbal art. And, related to this, Foley also argues that a traditional work of verbal art relies on the connotative value of its language compared to its denotative value, more so than its literary counterparts. Foley encapsulates these ideas in the phrase "traditional referentiality":

> If traditional phraseology and narrative are conventional in structure, then they must also be conventional in their modes of generating meaning. That is, at least part of the answer to the question of "how" these elements function is "in the same way each time." There will of course be room for the individual poet to contribute to the negotiation of meaning, the relative importance of that contribution depending on factors such as the idiosyncrasies of each tradition, genre, and text. But by and large the referential function of traditional units will remain consistent, everything else being equal. (1991:6)

In other words, oral performers are certainly able to bear their own influence over the traditions they perform. However, they are also able to rely on their audiences to understand their oral text in light of the preexisting, circumambient tradition that provides the essential context within which the text acts as a vehicle for communication. The circumambient tradition is the enabling referent to which the oral performance refers.

From traditional performance to traditional text

We acknowledged early in Chapter One that students of the NT never analyze actual oral performances of the Jesus tradition. We only ever deal with written texts. By definition first-century performances of the oral Jesus tradition no longer exist, and students confined to the twenty-first century can only gaze upon the written remnants of the tradition and wonder how the earliest Christians experienced the tradition in all its multisensory fullness. New Testament media critics will always be confined to researching written texts, the isolated, decontextualized, two-dimensional remains of once vibrant and fully experiential events. Once again, John Miles Foley proves to be a useful resource as we try to appreciate and account for the oral Jesus tradition in our analyses of the written Jesus tradition.

Foley regularly refers to "oral-derived texts," written texts that have "roots planted firmly in an oral tradition" (1995a:xi). We should not think of oral tradition as a source lying behind oral-derived texts.[38] Instead, oral tradition in this model provides the *context* in which the oral-derived texts developed and were experienced by their readers and/or audiences. More importantly, flesh-and-blood audiences receive and interpret oral-derived texts within the shadow of their experiences of the oral performance of the tradition. Foley specifically asks "how a given text continues [its] tradition of reception" (1995a:79) and proposes three factors that contribute toward an answer: performance arena, register, and communicative economy (1995:79–95; see Rodríguez 2010:97–102). The modulation from oral performance to written manuscript does signal an important moment in the media history of a tradition. But readers who have personal experience with the nonwritten oral performance of the tradition—both lectors and audiences of public readings—will receive and interpret the written text as yet one more instance (or one more performance) of the tradition rather than as the definitive, singularly authoritative expression of that tradition.

Consider the near-universal consensus that the authors of Matthew and Luke used the Gospel of Mark as a written source. If so, we can see immediately that neither Matthew nor Luke perceived the written text of Mark as a fixed, unchangeable account of Jesus' life and teaching. They preserved the larger structure as well as many of the details of Mark's narrative, and so they apparently approved of the Markan "performance" of the tradition. Nevertheless, both Matthew and Luke rearranged, condensed, expanded, and integrated Markan material with other traditions available to them. In other words, they received Mark as an *instance* of the Jesus tradition, an instance that neither fixed the structure or contents of the tradition in written form nor forestalled other performances of the tradition. Both Matthew and Luke provide a glimpse of what it means for us to conceive of Mark as an oral-derived text.

Readers and audiences depend on "extra information" in order to properly interpret and understand oral-derived texts. "[C]ontexts that lie outside the received version or text are most certainly active and crucially important, both for the performer/writer and for the audience, and interpretation requires consideration of those engaged contexts" (Foley 1995a:xi). As a result, when media critics lament the loss of oral tradition,[39] we ought to realize that we have lost the *context* in which our oral-derived texts were composed, performed, received, and interpreted by real people in antiquity more than the *source* of those texts. The people behind our written texts—authors, lectors, oral performers, as well as their audiences— regularly and repeatedly experienced the Jesus tradition in verbal form, with or without a written text, with or without someone on hand to physically read from a written text. Moreover, those regular and repeated experiences with the Jesus tradition affected the way these people—authors, lectors, oral performers, as well as their audiences—perceived, experienced, and interpreted the written texts and their public readings.

We can explore this point a bit more concretely. When an early Christian audience heard a performer (or lector) say, "The beginning of the good news of Jesus Christ, the Son of God" (Mk 1.1), that audience's entire history of experience with the Jesus tradition enabled them to access larger traditional associations (or connotative significances) that such meaningful phrases as "good news," "Jesus Christ," and "Son of God" open up (unless this really was their first hearing of the story of Jesus). The oral expression of a Markan narrative, with or without a written text, involved the presence and active participation of at least one person, the performer or the lector, who could accommodate the needs of the audience (whether they were more or less familiar with the Jesus tradition, whether they were enthusiastic or skeptical, etc.). In other words, the context of an oral performance of the Markan tradition—whether reading the Gospel of Mark or telling its story without actually reading the written text—always involved an element of human interaction. That interaction enabled the words of the performance to perform their connotative functions (i.e.

to carry more than their denotative meanings) even for relatively newer members of the audience.

The written text of Mark, however, was susceptible to decontextualization, to being removed from any meaningful context and being picked up in a completely alien environment. Imagine a copy of Mark's written Gospel winding up in the hands of a person who knows nothing about Jesus or his followers other than what she reads in the text and, perhaps, popular rumors.[40] Without a person to explain the language, imagery, and implied meanings (e.g. the traditional significance of the desert and the voice crying out, the prophetic resonances of the Baptist's diet and attire, or the biblical allusions in the words of the voice from heaven), the written text of Mark has lost its vital context that gives the Gospel its meaning, significance, and power. The reader who lacks access to the larger tradition has to work much harder to notice and take advantage of the rhetorical strategies by which the text signals its embeddedness in a particular tradition. And even then, this reader cannot expect that she has fully uncovered how the text strikes resonances and allusions to its circumambient tradition.[41] The written text facilitates these resonances and allusions, but it cannot force them upon ill-equipped readers.

This potential decontextualization is one of the primary effects of writing upon the Jesus tradition. In all probability, however, the earliest instances of the written Jesus tradition were typically experienced in the context of the enabling Jesus tradition and within the earliest Christian communities. If the earliest written texts of the Jesus tradition functioned within the same or similar social contexts as the oral Jesus tradition, this stability enabled the oral-derived text to continue the oral tradition's "tradition of reception" (Foley 1995a:79). The written tradition *could* escape that context and find itself subject to misreading and misunderstanding (or perhaps just *different* readings and understandings), but it did not *normally* escape that context.

I want to make one last point before we move on to consider how an oral-derived text's social context facilitates the tradition's continuity of reception. In 2010, I sat in on a meeting that considered whether the double tradition (i.e. material common to Matthew and Luke but not Mark, which most NT scholars attribute to a hypothetical document, Q) was oral or written. After one of the papers, during the question-and-answer period, I overheard one prominent Gospels scholar complain, "I don't see what's 'oral' about the Q-document."[42] According to the contextual approach to oral tradition and the NT, "oral tradition" refers to the oral-derived text's encompassing tradition. This circumambient tradition provides the context that enables an oral-derived text to convey its meanings to and perform its functions within early Christian social contexts. Oral tradition in this sense is a source for the written text, but it is more than that. It describes the multisensory, multilayered, totalizing social context that enabled the early Christians to interpret and respond to their written texts. What is "oral" about the written NT texts and their sources? Only their prewritten development, their communal expression, their exposition, their influence on later written texts and oral performances, and other things besides.

Word-power and the oral-derived text

In the discussion thus far, two factors have been especially significant, whether or not their significance has been explicit. First, and most obviously, we have highlighted the role of *tradition* as the context that renders a verbal message (oral or written) meaningful. Second, and perhaps less obviously, we have emphasized the role of *performance* as the event in which a verbal message finds expression and mediates the interaction of performer (or lector) and audience. "Performance" in this sense refers to the expression of tradition before an audience, either an extemporaneous recitation of an oral tradition or a dramatic and interpretive reading of a written text. Written texts did not communicate their contents apart from the act of reading, and reading in antiquity was usually done aloud (not always, but usually).[43] More than that, reading was often a performative event, including dramatic gestures, emotive pacing and intonation, and so on.[44] A lector mediated a written text's contents by performing the text, and the performance event is an important factor in how the text communicates its meaning to its audiences.

Foley repeatedly refers to "*performance as the enabling event and tradition as the enabling referent*" (1995a:28; italics in the original). We begin to get a sense of how traditional words, whether oral or written, function as communication when we pay attention to both performance and tradition.

> Empowerment of the communicative act results from the keying of performance—whether in the first instance by an actual experienced event or in the textual instance by its rhetorical vestige—and from the shared immersion in traditional context that is the performer's and audience's experiential heritage. (28)

When we neglect either performance or tradition (or both!), when we "reduce experiences to texts" (28), we lose the overwhelming majority of the early Christians' experience of the Jesus tradition, and we strip our texts of most of their power.[45] We lose our texts' *word-power*, their ability to "engage contexts and mediate communication" (1) in specific contexts, to specific audiences, using specific words, phrases, images, and themes. Word-power is the ability of traditional terms, themes and story-patterns to make reference to the tradition efficiently and effectively.

I have already mentioned three aspects of traditional verbal art that contribute to their word-power: performance arena, register, and communicative economy.[46] When we talk about an actual oral performance of the tradition, the **performance arena** refers to the location "where the event of performance takes place, where words are invested with their special power. . . . a recurrent forum dedicated to a specific kind of activity, a defined and defining site in which enactment can occur again and again" (47). When the tradition is written down (say, as the Gospel of John), the written text may be read within the "recurrent forum" of the performance arena, but of course it need not be. "The 'place' where the work is experienced by a reader, the event that is recreated, must be summoned solely by textual signals" (80). I object to the word "solely." Some written texts, including the Gospels, were likely read within the same or similar ritual and communal contexts as the prewritten oral tradition. Contemporary readers, however, do indeed rely completely on textual signals to perceive and approximate the appropriate context for reading the text. The performance arena does not merely identify the "place" where oral traditions are performed (or oral-derived texts are read).[47]

The performance arena frames the entire performative experience, whether an actual oral performance or a reading of an oral-derived text. We catch a glimpse of how an oral-derived text signals its performance arena in the prologue to John's Gospel. For an audience with ears to hear, the phrase, "In the beginning was the Word," calls to mind the entire Johannine tradition. More than that, "In the beginning" frames the Johannine tradition itself within the tradition of God's creative power (see Gen. 1.1), and the text reinforces this framing by echoing God's first creative act (Gen. 1.3–5; see Jn 1.4–10).[48]

Let us return to consider the dynamics of an actual oral performance of a tradition. When an experienced performer and an audience "with ears to hear" enter the performance arena, they speak in a dedicated **register**, a language or idiom that transcends the everyday, denotative meanings of its words and begins to emphasize their connotative significance or "institutionalized meanings" (Foley 1995a:50).[49] As we move from oral performance to oral-derived text, the textual exegete faces the challenge of identifying and appropriately interpreting the dedicated idiom—the register—of traditional performance inscribed on the written page. The specific features unique to traditional registers will vary from tradition to tradition. Examples may include archaic language or unusual grammatical or syntactical structures, paralinguistic cues, parataxis, rhythmic or rhyming schemes, and others. Examples of cues that may signal a traditional register might include the distinctive use of the historical present (especially in Mark) or of repetitive sounds (e.g. Mt. 5.3–10), among others.

The third aspect that facilitates the word-power of oral traditional messages is **communicative economy**. "Communicative economy" refers to the referential power of the dedicated register used within the circumscribed social environment of the performance arena (whether actual or rhetorical). In an actual oral event, both performer and audience join together in the performance arena to communicate traditional messages, messages that are not defined simply by their content but also by their idiom (= register). This idiom facilitates communication with comparative efficiency. It enables the audience that is already familiar with the tradition to fill in narrative gaps or make connections that, from a narrowly textual perspective, are not present within the text. For both the performer and the audience, however, the connections are as real as the textual signals that facilitate those connections.

As we shift from the event of oral performance to the rhetorical dynamics of oral-derived texts, the written text has to signal for its readers how it evokes its larger tradition. But even in the oral-performative act of reading, a lector and audience familiar with the oral tradition can employ the traditional connections in their reception of the oral-derived text. In other words, the informed audience's reception of the oral-derived text continues to resonate connections with its enabling referent (= its tradition) despite the fact that, for the modern critic, the text may only weakly summon its connotative referents (if at all). For example, we have already discussed the connotative associations of the Greek word *kyrios* ("lord"), which in certain contexts could refer to Jesus without any "value-added signification" (e.g. Jn 4.11, 9.36; see Foley 1995a:28) but in other contexts refers emphatically and exclusively to Jesus (e.g. Jn 20.28). The efficient and effective communicative economy of the oral traditional register only "works" when *both* the performer (or lector) and the audience are sufficiently fluent in the register. As a consequence, since contemporary readers (including NT scholars) are neither fluent in the traditional register nor experienced in the traditional performance arena, we can only detect the traditional idiom's communicative economy imperfectly and with considerable effort. But the authors and audiences of our oral-derived texts received the written texts from a perspective informed by their experience with the oral performance of the Jesus tradition. We need to be sensitive, therefore, to what evidence still exists that suggests how the authors, lectors, and audiences might have made connections between the text itself and the larger Jesus and biblical traditions that encompassed the performative event.

Within the enabling event of performance, the language used to express tradition shifts from the unmarked meaning of everyday speech to the special, "value-added" meaning of the traditional register. Whether the experience is real (an actual performative event) or rhetorical (mediated through an oral-derived text), the text's language takes on additional communicative economy, facilitating connections with its circumambient tradition—the oral-derived text's enabling referent.

Oral-derived texts: The model

Foley offers a model that charts potential differences between different kinds of oral-derived texts, from actual oral performances to authentically literary texts (see 2002:38–53; 2006:137). Foley's model expands our focus beyond the composition of written texts to also consider how those texts were performed and received by actual people (see Table 4.3). The row across the top asks how a work of verbal art is composed, performed, and received. The column on the left identifies different kinds of verbal art, though with the caveat that these are not four categorically distinct phenomena. For example, the difference between "Oral Performance" and "Voiced Texts" may blur in some instances.[50]

TABLE 4.3 Foley's model of oral and written traditional verbal art

	Composition	Performance	Reception
Oral Performance	oral	oral	aural
Voiced Texts	written	oral	aural
Voices from the Past	oral/written	oral/written	aural/written
Written Oral Poems	written	written	written

First, Oral Performance refers to a work of verbal art in which the written text plays no role whatsoever (unless a recording or transcription is made after the fact). In Oral Performance, the "text" is never written down but rather is summoned from memory, refashioned and retold in the present.[51] Anthropologists and ethnographers study Oral Performance in cultures around the world, but scholars of the NT and Christian origins simply do not have any access to the Jesus tradition as Oral Performance. We cannot even know *if* the Jesus tradition ever existed as Oral Performance, whether or not written notes, scripts, or whole texts always played a role in the performance of the Jesus tradition. Most media critics (myself included) assume the Jesus tradition was written down later, secondarily, after a period of purely oral expression, and we have reasons for this assumption. However, the data is far from conclusive.

A work of verbal art need not be composed orally, in the presence of an actual live audience, in order to be intended for (and most authentically experienced in) oral performance. A text may be written beforehand, perhaps memorized, and performed before an audience. Foley refers to these types of verbal art as Voiced Texts, which "aim solely at oral performance and are by definition incomplete without that performance" (2002:43).[52] In less technical language, Voiced Texts are scripts, texts that lead to an oral performance, whether through rote memorization, dramatic or emotive reading, or an interpretive retelling. The Gospels may have been written as Voiced Texts, as written documents that were intended for oral performance and that are incomplete apart that performance.[53] Paul's letters almost certainly were. Public readings of Paul's letters were, apparently, "weighty and powerful" (2 Cor. 10.10), and their author must have intended such a response. Until the act of public reading before their intended audiences, Paul's letters were incomplete.

The third classification, Voices from the Past, refers to "those oral poetic traditions that time has eclipsed and which we can now consult only in textual form" (Foley 2002:46).[54] Written texts that preserve once-oral traditions may have been composed orally or textually (or perhaps both). They may also have been accessed through oral performance, public reading, or private reading (or all three). Consequently, they may have been received aurally or as written texts. The flexibility of this third category results from our ignorance more than any desire to include as many phenomena as possible.[55] Given how little we know of the production, performance, and reception of the Gospels, I prefer to identify them as Voices from the Past rather than as Voiced Texts. In light of the striking similarities and differences between the synoptic Gospels as well as their relationship with other Gospel-texts (especially John and *Thomas*),[56] both oral and written media contributed to the composition (as well as the performance and reception) of the Gospels. The flexibility of Foley's Voices from the Past seems especially appropriate.

Finally, Foley refers to Written Oral Poems, an oxymoronic label acknowledging that, sometimes but not always, the shift from oral to written media can fundamentally transform the composition, performance, and reception of traditional material. Unlike the flexibility of Voices from the Past, Written Oral Poems are oral-derived texts written by an *author* for a *reading* audience. Their contents were composed apart from the influence of previous oral performances, and they are intended as literary works for readers who are not immediately available to or present with the author. Written Oral Poems often bridge the gap between a fading oral tradition and a literate audience with a cultural or antiquarian interest in that tradition. They are written for readers who are not themselves familiar with either the enabling event of performance or the enabling referent of tradition. However, they may transcribe genuinely oral tradition or compose new material in imitation of oral tradition.

For various reasons I would identify the written Gospels as Voices from the Past and the NT letters (both Pauline and General) as Voiced Texts. The precise dynamics of, for example, Matthew or Romans still require careful analysis, and we would still have to consider the different ways each NT text uses written and oral sources, interacts with other written and oral works, signals its performative expectations, and so on. Moreover, the remaining NT texts—I have in mind especially Acts, Hebrews, and Revelation—require individual attention to determine where (and whether) they fall within Foley's model of oral-derived texts. In the next chapter, I will offer some suggestive comments on various texts from the NT to demonstrate the consequence of approaching the NT corpus as a collection of oral-derived texts. I hope that these brief comments illustrate the potential payoff when we locate our written texts within a more nuanced and historically responsible media context.

CHAPTER FIVE

The *why* of oral tradition and NT studies

The previous chapters introduced the field of media criticism and oral traditional scholarship. In addition, they suggested some ways this scholarship intersects with the study of the NT. New Testament scholarship is ultimately concerned with historical, literary, and theological interpretation of a small group of texts. Therefore, any interdisciplinary contribution to NT scholarship will have to demonstrate how it opens up fresh perspectives on and interpretations of the Gospels, Paul's letters, and the other early Christian literature. In this final chapter, we will offer brief exegetical discussions of passages from four different sections of the NT canon.

Casting Jesus out into the wilderness

Immediately after Mark narrates Jesus' baptism, he briefly refers to Jesus' temptation in the wilderness. The New Revised Standard Version (NRSV) translates Mk 1.12–13: "And the Spirit immediately drove him out into the wilderness. He was in the wilderness forty days, tempted by Satan; and he was with the wild beasts; and the angels waited on him." The phrase "drove out" in v. 12 translates the Greek word *ekballō*, which can be used to describe forcible compulsion ("force to leave") but can also describe sending or bringing something out without the connotation of force.[1] Commentators have found Mark's choice of *ekballō* striking, however, because it often occurs in the context of an exorcism to describe the forcible expulsion of demons and/or unclean spirits from a person possessed. Mark's word choice stands out even more because Matthew and Luke, in their accounts of Jesus' temptation, use variations of a less marked word (Matthew uses "led up" (*anagō*); Luke uses "led" (*agō*)).

Craig Evans explains the differences between Mk 1.12 and Mt 4.1|Lk 4.1 in terms of Markan priority and Matthew's and Luke's "stylistic improvements upon Mark" (2004:5–6). According to Evans, when Mark wrote that Jesus ventured into the wilderness under inspiration of God's Spirit, he used the relatively marked word, "drove" (or "cast out"; *ekballō*). At some later point, first Matthew and then Luke set out to write their own Gospels. When they read Mark's striking phrase, "And immediately the Spirit cast him out into the wilderness," Matthew and Luke independently chose to use less marked language, so that Jesus "was led up into the wilderness by the Spirit" (Mt. 4.1), or he "was being led by the Spirit in the wilderness" (Lk. 4.1). Evans finds this scenario much more plausible than the alternative, that Mark saw Matthew's and Luke's "led [up]" and made the editorial decision to use the more difficult language of "casting out."[2]

I agree with Evans that Markan priority—the theory that Mark was written before Matthew and Luke and that the latter two used Mark as a written source—provides a more coherent explanation of the synoptic Gospels' similarities and differences than does the Owen-Griesbach Hypothesis (the theory that Mark was written after Matthew and Luke and used the latter two as written sources). Even so, Evans' explanations of all three texts (Mk 1.12; Mt. 4.1; Lk. 4.1) are unconvincing. In other contexts, both Matthew and Luke use *ekballō* to describe the same or similar kinds of action as Mk 1.12, so we have no reason for thinking that either author would have perceived *ekballō* in Mk 1.12 as a poor word choice.[3] But Evans' explanation of Mark is even worse:

> Mark 1:12 is Mark's first use of *ekballō*. *It did not occur to him that he would subsequently use this word in reference to exorcism* [my emphasis]. Had the Evangelist narrated (or *read* in Matthew or Luke, if we accept the Owen-Griesbach Hypothesis) one or two exorcisms *before* narrating the temptation, he too

may have chosen a different verb, as Matthew and Luke would later do. (2004:6)

Is it really likely that Mark did not know that *ekballō* conveyed strong exorcistic connotations and would not have used it at 1.12 if he had?[4] Since Mark uses *ekballō* so prolifically in exorcistic contexts, we can be fairly confident that, already in 1.12, Mark knew that *ekballō* could mean, "to cast out," or even, "to exorcise."

Perhaps media criticism and its insights can help us here. A number of textual features suggest already that Mark has entered—rhetorically rather than actually—the performance arena and has switched to the dedicated register of his tradition. The mention of "the beginning (*archē*) of the gospel" (Mk 1.1) makes sense on a strictly textual, denotative level. That is, this is "the beginning" of the narrative of Jesus' life and teaching, which Mark calls a "gospel" (*euangelion*). However, for an audience with ears to hear, the Markan incipit (as Mk 1.1 is often called) strikes resonances with Hebrew biblical tradition.[5] The Book of the Twelve opens with the prophecies of Hosea, and the book of Hosea opens with two introductory sentences. The opening of Mark's Gospel echoes the second of Hosea's introductory sentences (see Table 5.1).

TABLE 5.1 Mk 1.1‖Hos. 1.2 [lxx]

Mk 1.1	Hos. 1.2 [LXX]
The beginning of the gospel (*archē tou euangeliou*) of Jesus Christ, the son of God.	The beginning of the word (*archē logou*) of the Lord, which came to Hosea.

The prophetic resonance of the beginning of Mark's Gospel becomes explicit in the second verse, which cites the written prophetic tradition and which specifies the Isaianic tradition as its traditional referent: "Just as it is written in the book of Isaiah the prophet" (Mk 1.2). Moreover, immediately after he names Isaiah the prophet, Mark famously goes on to cite not Isaiah but Malachi (the last prophet included in the Book of the Twelve; see Table 5.2).

TABLE 5.2 Mk 1.2||Mal. 3.1 [lxx]

Mk 1.2	Mal. 3.1 [LXX]
Behold, I am sending my messenger before you, who will prepare your way.	Behold, I am sending out my messenger, and he will attend to the way before me.[6]

Commentators often focus on the difficulty of the fact that Mark refers to Isaiah but quotes from Malachi, and understandably so (see Yarbro Collins 2007:136). But we should not miss the effect of Mark's "error":[7] In his opening three verses, Mark resonates with the opening of the Book of the Twelve (v. 1), mentions Isaiah's written prophecy by name, alludes to the closing chapter of the Book of the Twelve (v. 2), and cites an actual Isaianic passage with considerable accuracy (v. 3). And, of course, Malachi's reference to Elijah (3.22 lxx) and Mark's application of Mal. 3.1/Isa. 40.3 to John will set the groundwork for Jesus' link between John and Elijah in Mk 9.11–13.

When Mark finally begins his narrative in v. 4, he has signaled to his audience the enabling referent of his performance: Israel's prophetic tradition. By the time John comes on stage, the prophetic tradition is fully present as Mark describes John, "baptizing *in the wilderness* and proclaiming a baptism *of repentance* for the forgiveness of sins" (Mk 1.4). The italicized phrases interact with their enabling referent to call much larger narratives to mind. These "larger narratives" include Israel's journey into the Sinai wilderness, the covenant with the Lord, and of course the covenantal consequences found, for example, in Deuteronomy 30.[8] Mark reinforces this traditional context in v. 6 by portraying John in Elijah's dress (Yarbro Collins 2007:145–6), which reactivates the Elijah resonance from v. 2. These observations on the opening six verses of Mark call into question the significance of claims that "Mark quotes relatively infrequently from the OT" (Edwards 2002:10).[9] More fundamental than the number of biblical quotations in Mark—a rather crude and blunt measure—is the narrative's connection to biblical tradition as its enabling referent. Indeed, Mark's account of Jesus' life and teaching draws its word-power from this enabling referent.

So how does Mark's modulation to the traditional register (with all the communicative economy of that register, as we have suggested for terms like "beginning," "wilderness," and "repentance" in vv. 1–4) and his rhetorical invocation of the traditional performance arena position us to understand the Spirit's strange "casting out" of Jesus into the wilderness in Mk 1.12?[10] First, we can say with complete confidence that Mark was already aware that *ekballō* could mean "exorcise," even though he had not yet narrated any exorcisms. Mark was, after all, an experienced performer of the Jesus tradition, and nothing warrants the assumption that the written Gospel of Mark was our author's first time hearing or performing his narrative. Second, we can probably say more than that the effect of Mark's word choice "is to make the temptation seem more of an unsought and uncomfortable experience, an ordeal" (Hurtado 1989:20). Other instances of *ekballō* obviously do not convey connotations of "an unsought and uncomfortable experience" (e.g. Mt. 9.38 par.). Moreover, we certainly would not want to suggest that Matthew and Luke sought to mitigate the temptation's "ordeal-ness" by using "led" instead of *ekballō*.

Some have suggested that Mark's use of *ekballō* echoes Gen. 3.24, in which God "cast Adam out [*ekballō*] and settled him opposite the garden" (LXX). According to this reading, Mark presents Jesus as a new Adam. However, Mark does not employ a new-Adam typology for Jesus anywhere else in the Gospel, and it would certainly be strange to parallel the Spirit's treatment of Jesus with God's curse on Adam. "Whereas God 'drove out' Adam from the garden *after* his temptation and disobedience, the Spirit 'drives out' Jesus into the wilderness *before* he is tested by Satan" (Heil 2006:64). Although this Adamic reading is clearly wrong, at least it attempts to situate Mk 1.12 within a larger traditional environment. Nevertheless, we need to see how (and why) the Adamic reading gets the specific target within that traditional environment wrong.

The better hearing of Mk 1.12 recognizes the echoes of Israel in Jesus' wilderness temptation. Exodus (LXX) uses *ekballō* some 14 times, all in a relatively coherent fashion.[11] First, we find some unruly shepherds "driving away" (*ekballō*) the daughters of the priest of Midian from a well until Moses arrives, rescues the women, and waters their sheep (Exod. 2.17). Nothing about Mark's narrative of Jesus evokes this episode, so we move on. The next five occurrences

of *ekballō* all concern Pharaoh's (and the Egyptians') eventual
"expulsion" of Moses and the Israelites from Egypt.[12] These five
uses of *ekballō* differ significantly from Mk 1.12. The people who
oppress God's people are doing the *ekballō*-ing in Exodus, whereas
in Mark the Spirit drives Jesus into the wilderness. We should note,
however, that YHWH himself says—even promises—to Moses,
"Now you will see the things I will do to Pharaoh, for with a
mighty hand he will send them out, and with an uplifted arm he
will expel (*ekballō*) them from his land" (Exod. 6.1 LXX). In other
words, Pharaoh drives out the Israelites *at* YHWH's *impulse*. The
final eight uses of *ekballō* in Exodus describe the Lord's promise to
"drive out" the nations from the land he promised to Abraham and
his descendants.[13] These also relate to Mk 1.12 only dimly. Now
God himself does the expelling (as in Mk 1.12), but those being
driven out are pagan gentiles, hardly an appropriate resonance for
the Spirit's act of driving *Jesus* out into the wilderness.

These results seem frustrating at first. In the story of the exodus,
the Israelites are driven into the wilderness. In the wilderness,
"testing" provides an important theme (e.g. Exod. 15.22–6;
17.1–7). However, none of the three uses of *ekballō* in Exodus—
the shepherds of Reuel's daughters; Pharaoh/the Egyptians of the
Israelites; the Lord of the gentile nations—parallel *ekballō* in Mk
1.12. And yet, if we can expand our vision beyond our strictly
textual frame of reference, we begin to see an important theme
emerge. In the very first use of *ekballō*, Moses "rises up" (*anistēmi*)
and "rescues" (*rhyomai*) Reuel's daughters. In the next five the Lord
provokes Israel's oppressors to expel his people from Egypt, which
elsewhere is described as an act of rescue (*rhyomai*; see Exod. 6.6;
12.27; 14.30). Finally, in the last eight uses of *ekballō* the Lord
promises to make the people's rescue complete by driving out the
gentiles from the land of Canaan in a fashion that leaves the land
fit for Israel to inhabit (see Exod. 23.29). As a whole, then, *ekballō*
occurs at every stage of YHWH's redemption of his people Israel
from the hand of Pharaoh.

Famously, however, Israel failed to rely on YHWH's power or
faithfulness to provide for and lead the people in the wilderness.
We ought to ask why Mark would use the same word—*ekballō*—to
narrate the Spirit's impulse on Jesus out into the wilderness. More
importantly, we ought to ask how an audience steeped in and

formed by the tradition of Israel's rescue from Egypt might have experienced Mark's use of the same word to narrate the Spirit's impulse on Jesus. The answer to both questions is: contrast. Israel, driven out into the wilderness for 40 years, faces testing and in turn tests the Lord,[14] and a generation falls in the desert. On the other hand, Jesus, driven out into the wilderness for 40 days,[15] faces testing by Satan and danger from wild beasts, and he emerges from the ordeal with the angels of the Lord serving him (Mk 1.12–13). In the Exodus tradition, *ekballō* summons the entire narrative of Israel's cries from Egypt, the confrontation between ẎHWH and Pharaoh, the escort out into the wilderness, and God's promise that he would clear the land as the people advanced. Mark taps this much larger narrative with extreme economy, indeed by simply using one unexpected word.

Before we move on to consider our next text, we ought to consider whether Matthew and/or Luke offer any confirmation of this reading of Mk 1.12. We have already objected to Hurtado's explanation of *ekballō* in v. 12 (that it "make[s] the temptation seem more of an unsought and uncomfortable experience, an ordeal"; Hurtado 1989:20), in part because of the implication that Matthean and Lukan redaction would then reduce the temptation story's discomfort. Does the media-critical reading we have offered avoid this problem? Since neither Matthew nor Luke use *ekballō*, both Gospels lose this highly economic, metonymic link with the tradition of Israel's wandering (= testing) in the wilderness. However, both evangelists counteract this loss by expanding their own performances of Jesus' temptation, explicitly and overtly citing the tradition of Israel in the wilderness three times![16] Whether Matthew and Luke decided independently to expand on Mark's account of the temptation (and so incorporated traditions from a now-lost source, which scholars refer to as "Q"),[17] or Matthew alone expanded on Mark and Luke followed Matthew,[18] we have evidence that very early readers of Mark recognized the function of Israel's exodus tradition—the enabling referent—as the context within which Mk 1.12–13 achieves its fullest and most meaningful interpretation. If Mark did not use the strange verb *ekballō* in v. 12 because of its traditional connotations, he could hardly have faulted his readers for activating those connotations in their reception of his performance.

Melding tradition in the Johannine prologue

In a recent essay on the Prologue of the Fourth Gospel (Jn 1.1–18), Tom Thatcher argued against the traditional view that these verses incorporate an older hymn. Instead, Thatcher argues that the Prologue is "the Evangelist's poetic expansion of a traditional saying associated with John the Baptist" (2011:30). He objects to the source-critical assumptions that have driven scholarly investigations of the Prologue, especially the premise "that the meaning of this text lies in the differences between the original source document and the Evangelist's adaptations of it" (36). Thatcher presses the media-critical principle of "equiprimordiality," in which "every oral text is a free-standing composition with a distinct identity and meaning" (39). The "original" text (or version) of the Prologue, which Johannine scholars have sought to reconstruct, never existed. Instead, every occasion on which the Fourth Evangelist spoke or wrote his account of the Logos and John's testimony on behalf of the Logos resulted in an "original" text (40–1). We cannot, therefore, speak of "an original Logos hymn" into which the Evangelist interpolated "alien lines" about John and his witness to the Light. "It would be more correct to say that the content of early hymns was always fluid, subject to the memory of the performer(s) and to the particular point that the performer(s) wished to make at any given moment" (41). If the Prologue's precise wording could fluctuate, with different performances incorporating or omitting certain lines, then we will have to look elsewhere for its stability.

Even when we take account of equiprimordiality, however, we can still recognize that traditional performers may take up traditional material—material with which the audience is already familiar—and apply it to a new context. Regarding John's Prologue, the Evangelist's audience "might simply note to themselves that John was singing the song a different way on this particular occasion" (41). All of this leads Thatcher to jettison the search for the original version of the hymn. More importantly, Thatcher shifts our focus from the Prologue's alleged disjunctive forces to consider how the Prologue's content explains and unpacks the traditional claim found in v. 15: that John testified on Christ's behalf, declaring the imminent arrival of one coming after John who was, nevertheless, before him. Thatcher's contextual—rather than disjunctive—reading of the Prologue resonates with Culpepper's description of vv. 6–8 as "a scriptural sounding introduction" to John the Baptist (1983:213), one that imitates biblical language.

Daniel Boyarin, like Tom Thatcher, doubts that the Prologue is an early hymn. He reads the Prologue as an interpretive reading ("midrash") of both Genesis 1 and Proverbs 8 (2004:93–105). He begins by briefly defining the Jewish interpretive practice of *midrash* as:

> a homily on a pericope, or extract from the Pentateuch that invokes, explicitly or implicitly, texts from either the Prophets or the Hagiographa (specifically, very frequently Psalms, Song of Songs, or Wisdom literature) as the intertextual framework of ideas and language that is used to interpret and expand the Pentateuchal text being preached. (95)

Midrashic practice, in other words, uses later scriptural texts (especially the Psalms, Song of Songs, and Wisdom literature) as a lens to view and interpret a text from the five books of Moses. It intentionally explores the connections between the biblical text and its circumambient tradition.

When we talk about midrash, we are talking about how an interpreting audience—in particular a Jewish audience—receives a biblical text: they do so in terms of the biblical tradition as a whole rather than in terms of alien, foreign, or otherwise extrabiblical ideas. "The first five verses of the Prologue to the Fourth Gospel fit this form nearly perfectly. The verses being preached are the opening verses of Genesis, and the text that lies in the background as hermeneutic intertext is Prov. 8:22–31" (95). As a result, the language and dominant themes of Jn 1.1–5 resonate with the creation tradition in Genesis 1, including "in the beginning," creation by spoken word, darkness/light imagery, and even certain structural features.[19] At the same time, these verses pick up a number of key themes and imagery from Proverbs 8 (LXX), including, again, "in the beginning," creation alongside (or through) Wisdom, and the presence of Wisdom with God. To the extent that Boyarin accurately describes scholarly interpretations of the Prologue as not having "explored in any depth the connection between Genesis 1 and John 1" (2004:94), these interpretations remove John's Prologue from its originating context—the tradition that is its enabling referent—and block its ability to communicate effectively and economically to its audiences. That is, they block its word-power.

Both of these analyses—Thatcher's reading of the Prologue as an expansion of a traditional saying about John the Baptist, and Boyarin's reading of the Prologue as a midrash on Genesis 1 and Proverbs 8—open up the connections between John 1 and its encompassing traditional context. Moreover, we can see how the Fourth Evangelist brings biblical tradition and the Jesus tradition in conversation with each other. Jn 1.1–18 is the product of the Evangelist's creative reformulation of a traditional saying from John the Baptist, which we find in v. 15. Thatcher repeatedly identifies v. 15 as a traditional saying, but he does not specify where else we might see this traditional saying (i.e. a saying common among Jesus' followers and not unique to the Fourth Evangelist or people associated with him). However, Jn 1.15 bears striking resemblance to a parallel passage in Mark (see Table 5.3).

To be sure, the Johannine saying has some striking differences from the Markan passage. In fact, Thatcher claims on the basis of these differences that, "the saying at Jn 1.15 appears to be the acoustic fulcrum of the Prologue's soundscape, the point where the primary unifying terms converge" (2011:47). Even so, we can still see the traditional nature of v. 15 in two areas: (1) the reference to someone "coming after me," which in the Gospels is both the crux of John's proclamation and a pointer to the imminence of Jesus' public ministry, and (2) the diminishing of John in comparison to the one who comes after him. We can be confident that the Evangelist was familiar with the saying in Mk 1.7, for he will

TABLE 5.3 Mk 1.7||Jn 1.15

Mk 1.7	Jn 1.15
And [John] proclaimed, saying, "He who is stronger than me is coming after me, the straps of whose sandals I am not worthy to stoop down and untie."	John is testifying about him, and has cried out, saying, "This is the one of whom I said: He who comes after me is ahead of me, because he was before me."

return to it at Jn 1.27, this time in a form more like its synoptic parallels.

If we follow Thatcher's lead, Jn 1.15's differences *vis-à-vis* Mk 1.7 are especially appropriate for its Johannine context. Thatcher identifies a number of "key words" in v. 15, key not because they bear robust theological significance but because they recur throughout the Prologue at very high frequencies. These words include "he was" (*ēn*), "become" or "he became" (*ginomai* or *egeneto*), and "come" or "he came" (*erchomai* or *ēlthen*), which are used nine, eight, and four times in the Prologue, respectively (see Thatcher 2011:43–7). Mk 1.7 only includes one of these words ("he is coming"; *erchetai*).[20] However, all three terms appear in the variant formulation of this tradition in Jn 1.15.

If, therefore, Jn 1.15 is a Johannine multiform of the traditional saying found in Mk 1.7, then the Fourth Evangelist has reshaped that traditional saying in order to fit its new performative context. Even if Thatcher is wrong to refuse a search for a pre-Gospel *Logos*-hymn behind Jn 1.1–18 (and I do not think he is), he has at least shown that v. 15 is thoroughly integrated into the Prologue. In fact, given the differences between Jn 1.15 and its Markan parallel (see Table 5.3), we probably ought to flip Thatcher's thesis on its head: not that Jn 1.1–18 is an expansion of the traditional saying in v. 15, but rather that v. 15 has been recast in terms more appropriate to 1.1–18. This accounts for v. 15's thorough integration into the Johannine Prologue, on the one hand, and its striking parallels with Mk 1.7, on the other.

If Thatcher's analysis demonstrates how the Johannine Prologue affected the shape of the traditional saying from the Baptist's preaching, Boyarin's analysis demonstrates how the biblical tradition of creation affected the shape of the Prologue as a whole. This in contrast to other popular readings, which emphasize differences between John 1 and Genesis 1 (e.g. Michaels 2010:46–7). Jn 1.1–5 provides a poetic interpretation of God's creation by the power of his spoken word (or Word): "And God said, Let there be light. And there was light" (Gen. 1.3). This word (or Word), in the beginning with God and as God, brings forth every aspect of creation (Jn 1.3), especially the life that is the light of humanity (v. 4). This strange phrase, "That which was in him was life, *and that life was the light of humanity*" (emphasis added), resonates with (and only makes sense in light of) the simultaneous evocation of Gen. 1.3

and 2.7. The same breath that spoke light into existence breathed life into humanity. This, then, is the creative word (or Word) of God.[21]

The Fourth Evangelist repeatedly acknowledges the failure of the darkness to comprehend the light (v. 5), of the world to know the true light (v. 10), and of his own to receive him (v. 11). It should surprise us at least a little bit that he never seems to feel the need to explain this failure. Instead, John (the Evangelist) uses the tradition of John (the Baptist) to address a problem that we might not immediately expect: Not, Why do people *reject* the Word/Light? but rather, Why does anyone *accept* the Word/Light of God? "John [the Baptist] himself will introduce his questioners to Jesus for the first time as someone 'whom you do not know' (1:26), admitting that 'even I did not know him' (1:31, 33)" (Michaels 2010:65). In the traditional world surrounding and inhabiting the Fourth Gospel, the normal, unmarked response to the Word/Light of God is unrecognition and rejection.

The Baptist, however, comes to reverse the situation and open a way for people to recognize the creative Word and revelatory Light of God. He comes as a testimony to the Light, to testify on behalf of the Light, that everyone might believe through his testimony (v. 7). But this revelatory function is not just important for the Prologue; it prepares the reader to understand the image of Jesus throughout the Fourth Gospel. "John's prologue reveals the identity of Jesus at the beginning of the story. As a result, the reader can discover hidden meanings and the recognition of suppressed signals behind or over the characters and events that appear later" (O'Grady 2007:220). The Prologue therefore provides essential information not just to inform the reader of certain facts (Jesus' identity, John's role, etc.) but to signal to the Johannine audience the kind of narrative to follow. That is, the Prologue establishes the Johannine narrative's biblical tenor and contributes to the overall connection between Moses and Jesus throughout the Fourth Gospel.

Rather than an oddly interpolated, cut-and-pasted-together text, which was then tacked on to the beginning of the Gospel of John, Thatcher and Boyarin have opened up a way for us to perceive and explore the Johannine Prologue's metonymic connections with its circumambient traditions, the silent but determinative associations that rendered Jn 1.1–18 a meaningful act of communication for its earliest audiences. As a result, we can make a number of additional connections between the rest of the Prologue, on the one hand, and the biblical and Jesus traditions that provide the Prologue's (and the Fourth Gospel's) essential, enabling referent, on the other.

First, the movement of the second half of the Prologue—from "his own people" (*hoi idioi*) who did not receive him to those who are now "children of God" (*tekna theou*) in vv. 11–12—parallels the narrative movement in biblical tradition following the Creation account. That is, in Genesis 3 the man and woman, created in the image of God, hide from God. In the subsequent narrative (Genesis 4–11), humanity's reception of God continues to degenerate. However, God speaks to Abram in Genesis 12, and Abram receives God's word and "believes" him (*pisteuō*; Gen. 15.6 [LXX]; see also Jn 1.12). By the time God moves to bring Abraham's descendants out of Egypt, he refers to them as "my firstborn son, Israel" (*huios prōtotokos mou Israēl*; Exod. 4.22 [LXX]). The point here is not that the Fourth Evangelist has Gen. 15.6 and Exod. 4.22 (or any other texts) in mind when he writes Jn 1.11–12. The point is that the Johannine Prologue and the Fourth Gospel as a whole explicitly evoke biblical tradition, and the movement in vv. 11–12 parallels the movement we find in biblical tradition. The relationship between these texts is *traditional*, not textual.

Second, the parallel movement continues past Jn 1.12. That is, after Abram "believes" God and God names Israel his firstborn son, he pitches his tent among his people, just as the Word "makes his dwelling among us" (*eskēnōsen en hēmin*) in Jn 1.14. J. Ramsey Michaels recognizes the traditional allusion here: "[T]he tent imagery evokes the Exodus, and the tenting of God with the people of Israel in their desert wanderings. This is evident in the close association of the phrase 'encamped among us' with the 'glory' (*doxa*) of the Word" (2010:79). Again, the Prologue's relationship with the Exodus tradition is not literary, as Michaels notes (79–80). Even so, the allusion in v. 14 is no less real. This allusion confirms our decision to read the Prologue in the context of Mosaic tradition. And, as O'Grady points out (2007:218), the glory "we have beheld" (1.14) appears again in John 17, when Jesus refers to "the glory I had with you before the world came to be" (17.5) and declares that he has given this glory to his followers (17.22). Even more significantly, Jesus prays that his followers would continue to see his glory by being with him (17.24); the intersection of both presence and observing glory is common to both 1.14 and 17.24. The movement we have been tracing through the Prologue, then, continues throughout the rest of the Fourth Gospel.

Finally, we can be sure that the reference to Moses in Jn 1.17 is not polemical and, in fact, is not even contrastive or adversative. The commentary tradition has often missed this. C. K. Barrett, for example, refers to "the contrast between Moses and Christ, Law and Gospel" (1955:169); so also does Bultmann (1971:78–9). More recent commentators have followed their lead (e.g. Morris 1995:99; Lincoln 2005:107–8; Michaels 2010:90–1; von Wahlde 2010:2.14 [?]). However, v. 17 simply makes two statements ("the Law was given through Moses; grace and truth came through Jesus Christ") and does not include any adversative conjunctions ("*but* grace and truth . . ."). When commentators read the two halves of v. 17 as opposed to each other, they are importing this opposition into the text. Up to this point, John has applied Mosaic tradition to Jesus (esp. concerning creation and the exodus), using this tradition as a lens through which to view and interpret Jesus' significance. Later, the Fourth Gospel informs his audience that Moses writes about Jesus (1.45; 5.46) and accuses Jesus' opponents (5.45). Nothing, then, justifies the conclusion that Jn 1.17 opposes "the Law" against "grace and truth." Instead, we have every reason to agree with those commentators who have resisted this adversative reading (e.g. Schnackenburg 1968:1.277; Beasley-Murray 1999:15; Köstenberger 2004:47–8). Though we still need to hammer out the details of the movement from "the Law/Moses" to "grace and truth/Jesus Christ," we need to do so without severing the connection between the text of the Prologue and its relationship with its circumambient tradition.

Hearing Moses preaching Christ

Thus far, we have considered passages from two very different NT texts: (1) the story of Jesus' wilderness temptation from one of the synoptic Gospels, and (2) the Prologue of the Fourth Gospel. Despite the broad similarities between these two texts—both are narrative Gospels, and both tell the story of Jesus, climaxing with an account of his execution and reports or accounts of his resurrection—the language, rhetoric, imagery, and presentation of Jesus differ sufficiently between Mark and John that we can probably justify dividing them into different aspects of early Christian literature (synoptic Gospels and Johannine literature, respectively).

In the present discussion, we will leave behind narrative Gospels completely and turn to another division of the NT canon: epistolary literature. As we move from narrative to epistolary texts, we will need to return to Foley's four-fold model of oral verbal art. The ambiguity of the categorization, Voices from the Past, with its noncommittal descriptions of a text's composition, performance, and reception (i.e. as "oral/written"), might tempt us to approach the NT epistles as Voices from the Past (as we did the Gospels). Three factors, however, suggest that we ought to reopen the question of the epistles' location on Foley's four-fold model. First, our knowledge of the epistles' composition, performance, and reception differs from our knowledge of the Gospels. Unlike the Gospels, many of epistles explicitly mention their author(s) and/ or their audience, even if only rhetorically.[22] We also have some indirect evidence for our epistles' composition, performance, and reception. For example, the description of Paul's *persona* as "weighty and powerful" (2 Cor. 10.10) strongly implies that the public reading performance of Paul's letters were expressive and rhetorically powerful (see Ward 1995).

Second, we can reasonably assume that Paul wrote (or dictated) his letters in order for them to be publically declaimed. They were, in a very real sense, "incomplete" until the act of public performance. "[T]hey are texts that originated as and were designed for oral presentations" (Botha 1992:21).[23] If so, we should consider Foley's description of Voiced Texts (composition: written; performance: oral; reception: aural). "Voiced Texts aim solely at oral performance and are by definition incomplete without oral performance. . . . only in the case of Voiced Texts is the spoken word the necessary and defining outcome of the composition-performance-reception process" (2002:43).[24] Unlike the written Gospels, whose traditional titles "present them as one gospel in four forms: *the* gospel according to Matthew, Mark, Luke and John" (Alexander 2006:14), each of the NT epistles only exists in one form, at least originally.[25] Consequently, the performance of, say, Romans necessitates a copy of the written text and a lector reading the text in a way that the performance of, for example,

Jesus' Sermon on the Mount does not require a written copy of Matthew (or Luke, or Q).

Third, unlike the Gospels, the NT epistles do not embody preexistent tradition. The written Gospels present themselves as portrayals of events and teachings that happened some 40 to 70 years before they were written down. And at least since the form critics scholars have acknowledged and investigated traditions contained in the written Gospels that predate the writing of the Gospels, including the series of five controversy stories in Mk 2.1–3.6, or two series of miracle stories in Mark 4–8, and so on. In other words, the Gospels embody and preserve traditions that existed before and apart from the Gospels in which they are now preserved. The NT epistles, on the other hand, come into being with the act of writing. Even if Paul incorporates material he had formulated beforehand into his letter to the Philippians, for example, the act of writing the letter puts traditional material into new contexts and applies them to a specific rhetorical situation.[26] The stories of Jesus existed before the written Gospels; the letters of Paul did not exist before they were written. We cannot, then, responsibly treat the NT epistles as Voices from the Past. Voices from the Past preserve traditions that were orally expressed before and/or apart from the written text. Instead, in the present discussion we will treat the NT epistles as Voiced Texts.

Finally, we will focus on a specific passage from Romans. Media-critical Pauline scholarship has not been as robust or prolific as its Gospels counterparts. The scholarship that has been done tends to focus on identifying oral features of Paul's letters (the morphological approach to oral tradition and the NT). Pauline media-critical scholarship has also focused on analyzing the presence, form, and function of Jesus traditions in Paul's letters, with special attention paid to Paul's use of "tradition-terms," such as "receive" (*paralambanein*) or "hand on" (*paradidonai*).[27] The current discussion, in contrast, will attempt to locate a Pauline text within its oral-traditional context, to identify how Paul's written text signals its metonymic references to its circumambient tradition.

In Romans 10, Paul gives voice to the Mosaic covenant, though previous media-critical discussions of Paul risk obscuring the media dynamics of this "giving voice" (e.g. Kelber 1983:155–9; Ito

2006). The problem stems largely from their too-sharp distinction between written and oral communication.[28] Paul writes,

> For, with respect to the righteousness that is revealed by the Law,[29] Moses writes (*graphei*), "The person who practices these things will live by them." But the righteousness that is revealed by faith speaks (*legei*) in this way: "Do not say in your heart, 'Who will ascend up into heaven' (that is, to bring Christ down)? or 'Who will descend into the abyss' (that is, to bring Christ up from the dead)?" But what does it [= the righteousness revealed by faith] say? "The word is near you, in your mouth and in your heart" (that is, the word of faith that we proclaim). For if you confess with your mouth that Jesus is Lord, and if you believe in your heart that God raised him from the dead, you will be saved. (Rom. 10.5–9)

Ben Witherington, along with many other Romans commentators, identifies "two different voices in vv. 5–7" (2004:261; see also Jewett 2007:622–3). If he is right that this text features "two different voices," this is the first time in Romans that Paul opposes Moses with Moses. The different verbs Paul uses in v. 5 and v. 6, whereby Moses "writes" but righteousness "speaks," might confirm that we are dealing here with two different voices, using two different media, which result in two different relations with God (see Table 5.4):

TABLE 5.4 The "Two Voices" of Romans 10.5–8

Moses	righteousness by faith
↓	↓
writes	speaks
↓	↓
righteousness revealed by Law	the word, in your mouth, in your heart
↓	↓
Judaism	Christianity

Despite the relative ease with which we can draw this dichotomy out of Romans 10, a number of reasons suggest that this is a fundamental misreading of Paul. First, elsewhere Paul insistently affirms Israel's sacred tradition. When his imagined interlocutor asks, "Do we then nullify the Law by our faith?" (Rom. 3.31), Paul exclaims, "By no means! Rather, we establish the Law." Paul would be utterly incoherent if, now, he were to distance himself from the same Law he earlier affirmed so emphatically.

Second, if Paul's aim in Romans 10 is to demonstrate the Mosaic Law's insufficiency, then it is altogether odd that he pulls the words that the personified Righteousness (*Dikaiosyne*) by faith speaks in vv. 6–8 from the Law of Moses, namely Deut. 30.11–14. If *Dikaiosyne* disproves and displaces Moses, why should she quote from Moses to define herself?[30] Third, despite the easy opposition between Moses "writing" (*graphei*) and *Dikaiosyne* "speaking" (*legei*) in vv. 5–6, we must recognize that Paul runs roughshod over this opposition just five verses later, when he presents Israel's sacred *written* tradition as speaking. "For the scripture (*graphe*) says (*legei*), 'Everyone who believes in him will not be put to shame'" (Rom. 10.11, quoting Isa. 28.16). In Romans 10, then, Moses, Righteousness (*Dikaiosyne*), and Isaiah speak with one voice. And when they speak, the words they speak are the written words of the covenant.

I think N. T. Wright has the better approach: "[I]t would be naive to think that Paul supposed, or imagined his hearers might be tricked into supposing, that Deuteronomy was not a book of Moses just as much as Leviticus was" (2002:658–9). Wright goes on to interpret Romans 10 in light of "the entire context of Deuteronomy 30." This is a move in the right direction, but he does not go far enough. Paul's point comes clearly into view when we appreciate the ways he draws on the *entire* tradition of the Exodus and the specific function of Deuteronomy 30 within that tradition.

The Exodus tradition begins with the unusual circumstances surrounding Moses' birth and with God's appearance to and commission of Moses (Exodus 1–3), in which Moses speaks directly to YHWH and YHWH speaks directly to Moses. This direct communication hearkens back to God's interaction with the Patriarchs, to whom God appeared (though without revealing his identity; see Exod. 6.3). YHWH shows himself to and speaks with Moses in ways that surpass YHWH's self-revelation and communication even to Abraham, Isaac, and Jacob. However, throughout the Exodus tradition, Israel never had this direct, unmediated interaction with God. The tradition even emphasizes the people's lack of direct access to God, so that they cannot even touch the mountain on which God descends (Exodus 19). In the early moments of the Exodus story, if we were to ask, "Who will ascend into heaven to retrieve it for us?" (Deut. 30.12), the clear answer would be: "Moses." This is true not just in the early moments of the Exodus story. Throughout the wilderness wanderings, Moses stands between Israel and YHWH, and anyone who opposes Moses soon wishes they had not (e.g. Miriam and Aaron in Numbers 12; Korah in Numbers 16).

At the end of Deuteronomy, as the Exodus tradition gives way to the Conquest tradition, the situation changes in a couple of ways. First, because of Moses' enigmatic sin, Moses and Aaron would not lead the people into the land of Canaan (see Num. 20.12). Moses' tenure as the intermediary between the people and YHWH is coming to its end. Second, Moses announces that YHWH will gather the people again and lead them back into the land of promise after they experience the covenantal blessing and curse, turn back, and obey all of YHWH's commandments (Deut. 30.1–10). And third, in the passage Paul cites in Romans 10, Moses tells the people that the distance that has separated them from YHWH—the distance he and Aaron have bridged—no longer applies.

> For this commandment, which I am commanding you today, it is neither excessive nor out of your reach. It is not up above, in heaven, so that you should say, "Who will go up for us into heaven and retrieve it for us? Then, after we hear it, we will do it." Neither is it across the sea, so that you should say, "Who will go across for us, to the other side of the sea, and retrieve it for us? Then, he will make it audible for us, and we will do it." The word is very near you, in your mouth and on your heart and in your hands, for you to do it. (Deut. 30.11–14 [LXX])

The gap between God and his people has been bridged, not by Moses and his brother but by the word of God, the commandment that "is neither excessive nor out of reach." For the first time in the Exodus tradition, as the people finally prepare to enter the land God promised their ancestors, YHWH declares the presence of his word not just among but *within* his people. "The word is very near you, in your mouth and on your heart and in your hands" (Deut. 30.14). Moses had already anticipated the possibility of this intimate relation (see, for example, Deut. 6.6, 11.18), but the current passage is nevertheless striking for its portrayal of intimacy between God and the people.

Within this larger "biosphere" of the Exodus tradition, Paul dictates to Tertius his letter for gentile Christians in Rome (Rom. 16.22). His lengthy argument that gentiles have been adopted into God's family without having to submit themselves to Torah's yoke came to a conclusion in Romans 8. Beginning in Romans 9 he anticipates the objection that, if the gentiles are in, God's promises to Israel appear unfulfilled. Israel is zealous for God and for Torah, but they have misunderstood Torah (10.2–3), especially Torah's function as a witness for the righteousness of God revealed by Christ's faithfulness (see Rom. 3.21–2). What, then, is the proper understanding of Torah? "For Christ is the *telos* of Torah, resulting in righteousness for everyone who believes" (10.4). Commentators have debated Rom. 10.4 at some length, especially whether Paul offers Christ as the *end* of Torah or its *fulfillment*.[31] But we should notice two things about the connection between the problematic v. 4 and Paul's discussion in vv. 5–8. First, almost immediately after identifying Christ as the "end" (*telos*) of Torah, Paul quotes from the end of the Torah (Deuteronomy 30). Second, Paul picks up on that passage from Torah that highlights the change in the people's relationship to YHWH, from a relationship mediated by Moses to one in which the word (*to rhēma*) of the Lord is very near the people, in their mouth and heart and hands. In the current passage, Paul offers a *pesher*-style interpretation of the end of Torah (see Jewett 2007:624–9) that puts Christ forward as the factor that results in Israel's new, unmediated relation with the Lord.

But even apart from the theological consequences of Paul's point in Romans 10, we should not miss the media dynamics of his rhetoric. According to Kelber, Paul objected to "the grammatological nature of the Law . . . [and] the objectification of the Law as *gramma*" (1983:158). In a similar vein, Joanna Dewey trivializes Paul's use of Israel's sacred *written* tradition:

While Paul is clearly influenced by Jewish understandings of God, history, and apocalyptic, he seems little concerned with the text as text. Paul can and does appeal to Scripture when it is helpful to support his argument, but it does not appear to be the foundation for his understanding or the constant reference point. (1995:53)

However, quite the contrary to both Kelber and Dewey, Paul's thinking about Jesus is constrained by his reading of Moses, every bit as much as Paul's reading of Moses is constrained by his thinking about Jesus. This is what it means to identify tradition—Hebrew biblical tradition as well as the emerging Jesus tradition—as the "biosphere" in which Paul lived and moved and had his being, the enabling referent in terms of which Paul's letter to gentile Christians in Rome achieved its historic (and history-changing) word-power. Paul does not quote Deuteronomy to oppose Moses, despite Witherington's claim that, "in a sense Moses is pitted against himself" (2004:262). In Romans 10, Paul demonstrates concretely what he meant back in Rom. 3.21–2, where he described the righteousness of God as "attested to by the Law and the Prophets" and revealed "by the faithfulness of Jesus Christ to everyone who believes." Paul is not opposing or subverting the written tradition of Moses. He is appropriating it for his proclamation of the gospel!

Inscribing Christ as king

For our fourth and final example of media-critical exegesis, we turn to an apocalyptic NT text. John's Apocalypse is a veritable treasure trove for media critics, most obviously because both oral and written media feature so prominently and explicitly in the narrative accounts of John's visions. Not surprisingly, we can see the interweaving dynamics of oral and written tradition throughout the text, for example, in the blessing at the beginning of the book: "Blessed are the one who reads (*ho anaginōskōn*) and those who hear (*hoi akouontes*) the words of this prophecy and who keep the things that are written (*ta gegrammena*) in it, for the time is near" (Rev. 1.3).[32] In the context of a public reading, the written text enables an oral performance of the tradition, so that the audience experiences the contents of the written prophecy by hearing it.

Moreover, passages like Rev. 1.3 suggest strongly that John's visions were meant both (1) to be written down and (2) to be read publicly. On the basis of this first point—that these words must be written—we can infer that the act of writing in no way represented a betrayal or transgression of an originally oral tradition.[33] On the basis of this second point—that these words must be read publicly—we can infer that the written account of John's visions were not intended for private, silent readers. The written text always had communal functions in view, especially to bring into being a community "who keep[s] the things that are written in it, for the time is near."

The language of writing and of written texts occurs throughout the book of Revelation. The verb *graphō* ("I write") occurs some 29 times in 28 verses, and the related verb *epigraphō* ("I inscribe") occurs once. Perhaps it should surprise us that the related noun, *graphē* ("writing," "scripture") never occurs, though Revelation still refers frequently to written texts. Three related words that all mean "book" or "[little] scroll"—*biblos*, *biblion*, and *biblaridion*—occur 28 times in 24 verses.[34] With all this writing and all these written texts, we should point out that Revelation refers to a reader only once (Rev. 1.3). However, there are nine references to someone "opening" (*anoigō*) a *biblion* or a *biblaridion*.[35] We should probably also mention Revelation 6–8, which narrate the dramatic opening of the seven seals of the scroll (*biblion*) introduced in Revelation 5. Thus, in addition to the single reference to a reader in 1.3, we have ten references to someone unrolling a scroll (or a scroll having been unrolled).[36] These ten references certainly imply someone reading or preparing to read a written text.[37]

I want to focus on the scene in Rev. 5.1–8, in which the lamb takes the seven-sealed scroll. David Aune links this scene with the divine origin of the revelation (Grk: *apokalypsis*) given to Jesus and communicated to his servants via angelic intermediaries (Rev. 1.1): "The Lamb's reception of the sealed scroll from the One seated on the throne in Rev. 5:7 is certainly an appropriate dramatization of this opening clause in the Apocalypse" (Aune 2006:196). He also identifies 4.1–8.1 as a narrative unit consisting of "a lengthy throne room scene in two parts" (198) followed by a lengthy account of the breaking of the scroll's seven seals.[38] The enthronement scene in chapters 4–5 has engendered considerable discussion, most of which lies beyond our purposes. Instead, I want to focus on the function and significance of the sealed *biblion* in 5.1–14.[39]

Discussions of the sealed scroll have understandably focused on a number of important questions, including whether John is describing a scroll or a codex, the dynamics and significance of ancient seals and sealed texts, the meaning of the number seven, the pericope's prophetic background, and so on. These discussions rightly emphasize the royal significance of the entire scene as well as of its major components. However, the unusualness of the written text's function as a royal totem goes relatively unremarked. This issue is easily obscured because the scene as a whole is so saturated with obvious royal emblems, from the throne and one seated upon the throne to the lion, his tribe (Judah), and "the shoot of David." Even the seals on the scroll connote royal significance. "[I]n later Israel those who possessed seals were primarily kings and officials. Seals thus might be considered tokens of royal and official dignity and a conveyance of power" (Stefanović 1996:133). Similarly, the signet ring was a royal emblem that could be referred to simply as "a ring" (*daktylion*), as when Pharaoh placed his ring on Joseph's hand (Gen. 41.42 LXX), or alternatively as "a seal" (*sphragis*), as when YHWH declares his choice of Zerubavel (Hag. 2.23 LXX). All these royal symbols dominating the vision in Revelation 4–5 threaten to overshadow the royal significance of the seven-sealed scroll itself.

I want to keep our focus on the scroll itself as an explicitly royal emblem. The words *thronos* ("throne") and *biblion* never occur together in the Septuagint, and in the NT they only occur together twice, both times in Revelation (5.1, 20.12).[40] On two occasions the Septuagint uses *archōn* ("ruler") and *biblion* in the same verse (Job 42.17; Dan 12.1 Θ), but in neither instance is the scroll an emblem of the ruler's authority. The language of kingship (*basileus* ["king"] and cognate words) occurs 78 times in the same verse with *biblion* and/or *biblos*. The vast majority of these are references to "the Book of the Events of the Days for the Kings of Israel and/or Judah," which clearly does not refer to a symbol of the king's authority. None of the other instances of *basileus*-language and *biblion* in a single verse refers to a specific emblem of the king's authority or sovereignty.[41] Kings and their entourages used books, and their deeds were written in books. But in no case does the book/scroll represent an emblem of the king's authority, sovereignty, or right to rule.

Ranko Stefanović begins "the search for the ancient antecedent to Rev. 4–5 where a 'book' and the throne converge" by turning to Deut. 17.18–20:[42]

> And it shall be that whenever [your ruler] sits upon his throne (*epi tēs archēs autou*; lit. "upon his power/beginning"),[43] then he shall write for himself this second account of the Torah into a scroll (*eis biblion*) from the Levitical priests. And it shall remain with him, and he shall read in it all the days of his life, so that he might learn to fear the Lord his God, to keep all these commandments and to do all these statutes, lest his heart become exalted above his brethren, or lest he turn aside from the commandments, on the right or on the left, so that he might remain in his kingdom (*epi tēs archēs autou*)[44] for a long time, he and his sons among the children of Israel. (LXX)

Stefanović argues that this text, along with 2 Kgs 11.12||2 Chron. 23.11 and parallels from the ancient Near East and Egypt, "show[s] that associating the king with a book or manual of instructions and regulations was known in the ancient Near East" (Stefanović 1996:234). Nevertheless, however much the written scroll may have functioned as a symbol of the king's investiture, a crucial distinction makes this an inappropriate parallel to the phenomenon we see in Revelation. In all of Stefanović's examples, the written text exercises authority *over* the newly installed monarch. For example, Diodorus of Sicily learned that "the conduct of the Egyptian kings was regulated 'by prescriptions set forth in laws, not only their administrative acts, but also that had to do with the way in which they spent their time from day to day'" (1996:231, citing Diodorus Siculus, *Bibliotheca historica* 1.240–1). In the same way, the king in Deut. 17.18–20 is obliged to keep the scroll (*biblion*) with him throughout the length of his reign, to have it read to him regularly, and to submit his exercise of royal authority to its commandments and statutes. The written scroll may function as a symbol of the monarch's authority over the people (*per* 2 Kgs 11.12||2 Chron. 23.11), but it did so by subjecting the monarch to the authority of the written scroll and, ultimately, to God himself.[45]

The situation could not be more different in the enthronement scene of Revelation 4–5. Stefanović identifies a number of parallels with ancient covenant-treaty forms in Revelation and argues, "Christ, the faithful witness and 'the ruler' (ὁ ἄρχων, 1:5), is in vassal position and is God's representative and covenant mediator" (1996:294). But this argument leads to some problematic judgments. For example, when he says, rightly, "Revelation contains both blessings for loyalty and curses for breaking the covenant" (295), Stefanović never explains how these blessings and curses apply to Christ-as-vassal. The obvious explanation, which Stefanović does not sufficiently appreciate, is that the blessings and curses do not apply *to* Christ; they are applied *by* Christ to the faithful and the disobedient, respectively. Or again,

> The subordinated vassal position of Christ is particularly signified by the constant reference to God the Father as the one sitting on the throne or to the throne as the Father's, signifying the throne as the symbol of God the Father's rulership. The throne and the Lamb (presumably Christ), although closely related (cf. 7:17), appear to be separated and distinct (cf. 7:9). Phrases such as ὁ καθήμενος ἐπὶ τῷ θρονῷ [*sic*] καὶ τὸ ἀρνίον ("the one sitting on the throne and the Lamb," 5:13; 6:16; 7:10) or ἐνώπιον τοῦ θρόνου καὶ ἐνώπιον τοῦ ἀρνίου ("before the throne and before the lamb," 7:9) clearly show that. (299)

Whether or not the throne and the lamb are "separated and distinct," they stand in the same relation to those who actually receive the covenantal blessings and curses. Every creature throughout the cosmos (5.13) and the innumerable multitude (7.9–10) give praise to the one seated on the throne as well as to the lamb. Conversely, the victims of the sixth seal receive the covenantal curses and plead to the mountains and to the rocks, "Fall upon us and hide us from the face of the one who sits upon the throne and from the wrath of the lamb" (6.16). As I said above, the lamb does not *receive* the covenantal blessings or curses; he *administers* them.

Craig Koester has a better grasp of the dynamics of Revelation's enthronement scene. God and the lamb together perform the covenantal suzerainty functions while the cosmos itself performs the vassal functions, and the vision in Revelation 4–6 climaxes with "all creation join[ing] in giving praises to God and the Lamb" (2001:72). Koester's description of the elders in chapter 4 contrasts sharply with the depiction of the slain lamb in chapter 5. On the one hand, the elders "direct attention to God's reign. Their thrones and their crowns are theirs not by right, but as gifts from God" (75). On the other hand, when John weeps bitterly that no one is able to open the scroll's seven seals, one of the elders consoles John and directs his attention to the lion of Judah, the shoot of David (v. 6). It is only at this point, after the elder has pointed out the lion to him, that John sees the slain lamb standing in the midst of the throne, surrounded by the four living creatures and by the elders (v. 7).

The scene draws other contrasts between the elders and the lamb. Unlike the elders, who *prostrate* themselves before the throne, the lamb *stands* in the midst of the heavenly worship. Unlike the elders, who *cast* their crowns before the throne, the lamb approaches the throne and *takes* the sealed scroll. John uses the perfect tense for the verb "takes" in v. 7 (*eilēphen*; lit. "has taken"), which has the effect of drawing our attention away from all the other details of the heavenly throne room and focusing it on the action of the lamb's taking the scroll (Aune 1998:354). The effect is compounded in v. 8, when John refers a second time to the lamb taking the scroll: "And when he took the scroll, the four living creatures and the twenty-four elders fell before the lamb, each one having a lyre and a golden bowl full of incense, which are the prayers of the saints."[46] The contrast, then, between the elders who *direct* worship toward the throne and the lamb who *receives* worship is both clear and striking.

Revelation 5 suggests another distinction between this sealed scroll and other, more ordinary functions of written communications between kings and their subjects. In standard communications, the seals vouchsafe the scroll's authenticity. Once a king or a ruler has impressed his signet ring onto the wax seal(s),[47] no one has the authority to break the seal(s) except the intended addressee. So Koester says:

> The seven seals on the scroll—like the seals that were placed on royal decrees, wills, and other official documents—imply that its contents are valid. . . . The seal ensured that the scroll truly declared the will of its author and that no one had altered the text. Only a person who had been properly authorized was to break the seals and open the scroll. (2001:76, 77)

On this model, God himself sealed the scroll, and the lamb was its true addressee. As the king, or suzerain, God sealed the scroll to guarantee the authenticity of its contents as he sends it to his vassal. When it is delivered, only the authority of the addressee can break the seals and open the scroll.

However, at least three features of the text suggest that Revelation does not adhere to this standard model of sealed royal decrees. First, as we have already seen, the lamb is not a vassal ruler to whom God, as suzerain, sends a communiqué. Instead, the lamb stands "in the midst of the throne" (*en mesō tou thronou*; 5.6), sits on the throne with God (3.21), and receives the worship of the heavenly court. The lamb rules *with* rather than *on behalf of* the one sitting on the throne. Second, the scroll is not addressed to the lamb. As the scene unfolds, the lamb systematically breaks each of the scroll's seven seals (6.1–8.5), but he never reads the text. The next time we see the scroll, an angel descending from heaven brings the now-opened scroll to earth, gives it to John, and tells him, "Take it and eat it" (10.9).[48] After he does so he receives another commission: "You must prophesy again about many peoples, gentiles, tongues, and kings" (10.11). The scroll, then, is addressed to the world ("many peoples, gentiles, tongues, and kings") and proclaimed (= "read") by John, who has literally internalized its words (see Ezek. 2.8–3.7).[49] Third, the authority to break the scroll's seven seals is found not in the scroll's recipient but in its author. As the lamb opens each of the first six seals, a scene of judgment and vindication ensues: judgment against the unfaithful and rebellious, but vindication and glorification for those who have died for their testimony (the fifth seal; 6.9–11). However, we find out in 6.16 that the seals unleash "the wrath of the lamb." The text clearly implies, then, that the contents of the seven-sealed scroll belong to both the one seated on the throne and the lamb. These three considerations—the lamb's coregency with God, the actual recipients of the scroll, and the specifically *authorial* authority to break the scroll's seals—make clear that the scroll in Revelation 5 functions in unusual and culturally surprising ways.

Despite the ultimate inability of his standard model of sealed scrolls to explain the enthronement scene in Revelation 5, Koester does point to a helpful clue that helps to unlock this scene. After he describes John's despair that no one anywhere could open the sealed scroll, Koester explains the ensuing scene in terms of "the difference between what is heard and what is seen":

> John *hears* one of the elders say that "the Lion of the tribe of Judah, the Root of David, has conquered so that he can open the scroll and its seven seals" (5:5). The image of a lion, which connotes power and majesty, is identified with Judah, the tribe from which kings came in the Old Testament. The book of Genesis said that "Judah is a lion's whelp" and that the "scepter shall not depart from Judah, nor the ruler's staff from between his feet, until tribute comes to him, and the obedience of the peoples is his" (Gen. 49:9–10). . . . . What John actually *sees*, however, is not a lion but "a Lamb, standing as if it had been slaughtered" (Rev. 5:6). The vision of the slaughtered Lamb is startling given the expectation that a lion would appear. (Koester 2001:77, 78)

James Resseguie also draws helpful attention to this pattern: "The alternation between seeing and hearing is a hermeneutical key in the Apocalypse" (2009:118). The precise function of this alternation remains open to interpretation, but that lies beyond the scope of the present discussion. Instead, I want to draw attention to the scriptural dynamics of what John hears and sees and to draw a conclusion about the place of the seven-sealed scroll in the aural-optical alternation.

As John weeps that no one throughout the created cosmos can open the scroll's seven seals and reveal its contents, one of the 24 elders consoles him: "Stop weeping. Look! The lion from the tribe of Judah—the shoot of David—has conquered [and is worthy] to open the scroll and its seven seals" (Rev. 5.5). The elder's two metaphors "are messianic and raise expectations among those familiar with the Old Testament of a deliverer who will establish God's reign through his mighty power" (Resseguie 2009:117). The lion from the tribe of Judah is a clear and universally acknowledged allusion to Jacob's blessing in Genesis 49: "Judah is a lion's whelp; from the prey, my son, you have gone up. He bows down, he lies down as a lion; And as a lion, who shall rouse him? The scepter shall not depart from Judah, nor the ruler's staff from between his feet, until tribute comes to him; and the obedience of the peoples is his" (Gen. 49.9–10 NRSV).[50] The image of the lion connotes power and authority to rule (Osborne 2002:253), and the association of the lion with the scepter and the ruler's staff extends the connotation even further.

John picks up on the extension of the lion's function as a metonym for power and strength (Resseguie 2009:117) by bringing Gen. 49.9–10 and Isaiah 11 in line with one another.[51] Isaiah prophesies judgment against Israel's enemies (specifically, Assyria; Isa. 10.24–6), promising that "the Sovereign, the LORD of hosts, will lop the boughs with terrifying power; the tallest trees will be cut down, and the lofty will be brought low" (10.33 NRSV). In the aftermath of the Lord's clearing of the forest, we find the familiar prophecy of renewed Davidic hegemony: "A shoot shall come out from the stump of Jesse, and a branch will grow out of his roots. . . . On that day the root of Jesse shall stand as a signal to the peoples; the nations shall inquire of him, and his dwelling shall be glorious" (Isa. 11.1, 10 NRSV). In case anyone missed not just the authoritative but even the *royal* significance of "the lion from the tribe of Judah," John makes that significance clear with the addition of Isaiah's botanical metaphor: The lion is the shoot of David, the one who reigns over the kings and lords of the earth.[52]

Famously, after John hears about the lion|root that has conquered, he turns and sees the slaughtered lamb, standing in the midst of the throne. As we have seen, commentators have universally noted this bait-and-switch and have commented extensively upon the announcement of the lion but the vision of the lamb.[53] "John has juxtaposed two symbolic descriptions in vv. 5–6, each representing a widely-known story" (Aune 2006:199). The "widely-known story" Aune mentions is the tradition—as enabling referent—that provides the appropriate context in which John's vision and the announcement of the lion but the vision of the lamb is unlocked and enables communication between John and his audience.[54] However, another switch (or perhaps "juxtaposition" is the better word) has also taken place. Now, instead of the scepter that traditionally accompanied the lion of Judah, the lamb approaches the throne and takes the sealed scroll. The scroll has replaced the scepter as the salient symbol of the lamb's royal dignity.[55] Unlike other kings of Israel, whose authority to reign over Israel was symbolized by their submission to the written text, John's vision of the seven-sealed scroll emphasizes the lamb's authority *over* (or better, exercised *through*) the written text. As the apocalyptic narrative unfolds, a mighty angel brings the now-opened scroll down to earth, where the divine voice tells John to take the scroll, eat it, and to proclaim its contents (Rev. 10.1–11). In contrast to Deut. 17.18–20, where the Israelite king is commanded to read the written text and submit himself to its dictates, John *and not the Jewish monarch* receives the command to read and publicize the contents of the scroll.

Thus far, our discussion of the enthronement scene in Revelation 4–5 has done more than trace the innovative function of the sealed scroll as a royal emblem, a replacement for Judah's scepter. We have also bumped up against the very real differences between "reading" as conceived in the book of Revelation and "reading" as conceived in contemporary Western cultures.[56] To be sure, "reading" in a contemporary academic context—which involves secluding myself in my office (or in the quiet of a public library or reading room), pouring over multiple texts and sources, paying close attention to a text's unique wording, and constructing a coherent meaning or set of meanings—can be just as bizarre to contemporary nonacademics as any ancient practice of "reading." Even today, "reading" means different things to different people and even different things in different contexts to the same person (Johnson 2010:9–14). Within a broader understanding of "reading," we can find cultural analogues for the activity of Rev. 1.3, in which "those who hear" provides the counterpart to "one who reads."[57]

But nothing in my experience of the Western cultural *koine* provides a useful analogy to the conceptualization of reading in Rev. 10.9–11. The mighty angel tells John to eat the now-open scroll, and when he does so he receives a further commission: "You must prophesy again about many peoples, gentiles, tongues, and kings" (10.11). Here the act of eating the written scroll provides an analogy for reading, in which the reader internalizes the contents of the written scroll. But "eating" is not simply a metaphor for memorizing the written text; it also connotes the divine necessity of John's prophetic proclamation of the scroll's contents (Grk: *dei prophēteusai*; Rev. 10.11). In this analogy, the written text disappears completely but reemerges in John's oral proclamation.

We have to ask whether the disappearance of the text is merely a result of our pushing the analogy of reading-as-eating too far, a signal that we have misapprehended what it means to "read" the seven-sealed scroll. But I do not think we have misread the dynamics of Revelation 10. John's commission "to prophesy" charges him with an emphatically oral (and oracular) rather than a textual responsibility. If John's commission involves any textual responsibilities, they are to write and protect the written text; he never receives any command to *read* the text.[58] Ezek. 2.8–3.7 exhibits the same dynamic: the prophet sees an open scroll, hears a voice telling him to eat the text, and then is told to speak to the children of Israel.[59] The entire sequence of events makes it difficult to avoid the conclusion that this conceptualization of "reading" does two things at once that contemporary notions of "reading" generally consider diametrical opposites. On the one hand, this conception emphasizes the presence, significance, and function of an actual written text. Neither John nor Ezekiel simply report or repeat some tradition or piece of news that also happens to be written down somewhere. They are explicitly employing a written text, with all its attendant physicality and materiality, and deploying its cultural significance as a written text for particular ends. And yet, on the other hand, the written text disappears and plays no discernible role in its public declamation. The prophetic herald receives his authority and authorization from the written text he has consumed, but his audience must rely completely on his authoritative *persona* apart from any written text that might corroborate his message.[60]

* * *

The previous discussion has set out to illustrate the kinds of contributions that media criticism can make to NT exegesis and scholarship by looking at four very specific texts: the earliest written account of Jesus' temptation in Mk 1.12–13, the merging of biblical and Jesus tradition in the Johannine Prologue (Jn 1.1–18), Paul's *pesher*-style reading of Deuteronomy and the Exodus tradition in Rom. 10.5–8, and the royal significance of the seven-sealed scroll in Revelation 5. Space prevents us from considering media criticism's potential contribution to other divisions of early Christian literature, both canonical (e.g. Hebrews) and extracanonical (e.g. the *Didache*, the *Protevangelium of James*, or the *Gospel of Thomas*). Media criticism offers us analytical questions and tools to help us situate the written textual remains of Christian history within a closer approximation of their historical contexts. Anthony Le Donne and Tom Thatcher (2011) refer to this approximation as "first-century media culture," which I think is certainly a better and more helpful term than the nebulous and ill-defined term "orality." By shifting our focus toward placing our extant texts within a reconstruction of their "media culture," Le Donne and Thatcher (and their contributors) appropriately frame the primary goal driving NT media criticism: to interpret and explain the function of our written texts within their originative contexts, including our texts' composition, performance, and reception (see Keith forthcoming).[61]

We should plainly admit that we are always only ever explaining the written remains of early Christianity. Even so, we legitimately speak of *oral* tradition, and this for a number of reasons. First, many of the heuristic models employed by contemporary NT media critics were developed for research among actual oral traditions, whether in the former Yugoslavia, in the diverse tribal cultures of Africa or southeast Asia, among urban American slam poets, or wherever. Second, we are genuinely interested in the way that the earliest Christians' holistic experience of their traditions—including their oral experiences—conditioned the composition, performance, and reception of written texts. And third, many media-critical analyses of written NT (and extracanonical) texts emphasize that the early Christians experienced these texts as oral phenomena, whether they heard a written Gospel performed in a ritualistic public reading or a rhetorical presentation of a Pauline epistle or whatever. The interest in oral tradition certainly opens up fresh perspectives on the written texts of early Christianity. But it never opens up access to actual oral tradition. As such, our discussion in this volume has consistently eschewed any search for oral tradition "in" the written texts and has focused instead on the function of written texts in (oral-)traditional contexts. Thus the value of the perspective advanced by Le Donne and Thatcher: our extant texts in their first-century media culture. Hopefully, the present volume has provided a useful guide for anyone interested in reconstructing that media culture and locating our texts within it.

NOTES

Preface

1 See the discussion of Mk 1.12 in Chapter 5.

Chapter 1

1 It took me a few months to realize that "oral tradition" and "oral history" are not the same thing. Students of each ask different questions of different data and employ different means to pursue answers. For a discussion of oral *history* and the NT, see Samuel Byrskog's *Story as History, History as Story* (2000).

2 Sometimes other books are included in the collections, whether books of the Hebrew Bible (= Old Testament) or other, noncanonical books. For example, in addition to the NT, the fourth-century manuscript Sinaiticus contains the Septuagint—the earliest Greek translation of the Hebrew Bible, as well as some other Greek texts—and a few nonbiblical Christian texts, including the *Shepherd of Hermas* and the *Epistle of Barnabas*. Since our focus here is on the NT, I will not mention when a manuscript includes other texts.

3 For all the talk of "oral tradition" in NT scholarship, we need to realize that very many disciplines that study oral tradition actually have access to the oral traditions they study. Anthropologists can (and do) travel to Yugoslavia, Ghana, New York, or wherever, to listen to, record, analyze, and report on the oral expression of tradition. By way of contrast, NT scholars currently lack the necessary technology to travel to the Roman-Hellenistic Mediterranean world to listen in on and study early Christian oral tradition directly. This is an important point that every study of oral tradition and the NT should acknowledge clearly and plainly.

4 Defining and assessing "literacy" is notoriously difficult; for the purposes of the CIA World Factbook, American literacy is defined as "age 15 and over can read and write." See www.cia.gov/library/publications/the-world-factbook/fields/2103.html [accessed October 8, 2012].

5   Harris 1989; Hezser 2001; Keith 2010. Of course, our analyses
    must recognize that there are different levels of literacy, from the
    ability to read one's name or make out a brief legal contract to the
    more professional demands of reading religious, philosophical, and/
    or literary texts (see Rodríguez 2009:154–6).

6   Oddly, Craffert and Botha begin their essay with the strange claim
    that "current scholarship is fairly unanimous that Jesus could read
    and write" (2005:5). Certainly a strong contingent of scholarship
    argues that Jesus was literate (at some level), but that contingent
    hardly justifies the label "fairly unanimous."

7   Some scholars (e.g. Joanna Dewey, or Richard Horsley) seem to
    assume that written texts were confined to the Jerusalem Temple
    (as well as "at least some Judean and Galilean towns"; Horsley
    2001:57) and wielded by economic, political, and religious elites
    against the majority of the populace (see Horsley 2001:57–61).
    However, despite the likelihood that the social *function* of written
    texts extended beyond the geographical *presence* of written texts,
    even rural Galilee appears to have had its share of writing and its
    consequences, as we will see presently.

8   Mk 12.10 (singular; cf. par. Mt. 21.42 [plural]), 24 (par. Mt. 22.29);
    14.49 (par. Mt. 26.54, 56).

9   See Jn 2.22; 5.39; 7.38, 42; 10.35; 13.18; 17.12; 19.24, 28, 36, 37;
    20.9.

10 For a very helpful discussion of "widespread textuality" even in the
    midst of a largely illiterate population, see Keith 2011a:85–8.

11 All references to the Apostolic Fathers follow the numbering system
    found in Michael Holmes' edition (Holmes 2007). Translations are
    my own except where noted otherwise.

12 See, for example, Loveday Alexander (1990), Pieter Botha (1993),
    Richard Bauckham (2006), as well as the texts (English, German,
    and Italian) listed in Holmes 2007:728–9.

13 "Although conclusions must be tentative, we can detect a cultural
    assumption of the first and second centuries that the production of
    a book was not an inevitable—*or even necessarily a desirable*—end
    in itself: books are secondary to oral teaching" (Botha 1993:752;
    emphasis added).

14 "[W]hen Papias speaks of 'a living and surviving voice,' he is not
    speaking metaphorically of the 'voice' of oral tradition, as many
    scholars have supposed. . . . [T]he saying about the superiority of
    the 'living voice' to books refers not to oral tradition as superior
    to books, but to direct experience of an instructor, informant, or
    orator as superior to written sources" (Bauckham 2006:27).

15 "In the first place, it is not oral tradition as such that Papias esteemed, but first-hand information. . . . Thus, when he contrasts oral and written testimony, Papias is not denigrating texts. Second, Papias himself wrote books and must have expected that what he wrote, drawing in part on the tradition he had received, would be read and valued by others" (Gamble 1995:30–1).

16 In the famous story of the woman caught in adultery (Jn 7.53–8.11), known as the *Pericope Adulterae*, Jesus twice stooped down and began to write in the dirt with his finger (Jn 8.6, 8). Other than this, no Christian tradition depicts Jesus as writing anything, and, of course, whatever Jesus may have written in the dirt has not survived. (Chris Keith [2009:241–4, 247–8] discusses third- and fourth-century CE texts that portray "a literate Jesus," but at least two of these texts [Legend of Abgar; *Narrative of Joseph of Arimathea*] do not portray him actually writing, physically inscribing letters onto papyrus or parchment. The other two texts [Adamantius' *Dialogue On the True Faith in God*; Aphrahat's *Demonstrations*] are less than clear.) For a thorough and very insightful discussion of the *Pericope Adulterae*, see Keith 2009.

17 James Crossley (2004) argues that Mark was written nearer 39–41 CE, fully three decades earlier than the traditional consensus among scholars! His dramatic proposal has not found many adherents, though Crossley's doctoral supervisor, Maurice Casey, incorporates this early date of Mark into his own book on Jesus (Casey 2010).

18 The corpus of 13 Pauline epistles is largely written to churches (in Rome, Corinth, etc.), though four are addressed to individuals (Philemon, 1 and 2 Tim., and Titus). See also the General Epistles (James, 1 and 2 Peter, Jude, 1–3 John), as well as the seven ecclesial letters in Revelation 2–3 and the Apostolic Decree (Acts 15.23–9), which was sent out from Jerusalem, especially to churches in Asia Minor. The letter of 1 *Clement* was also written by the end of the first century; the *Epistle of Barnabas* may have been as well. Within the first two decades of the second century Ignatius, bishop of Antioch in Syria, wrote seven letters (six to Asian and European churches and one to Polycarp, bishop of Smyrna (on the western coast of Asia Minor)).

19 For example, the *Didachē* (lit. "The Teaching," a shortening of the document's traditional name, "The Teaching of the Lord to the Gentiles by the Twelve Apostles") may have been compiled by the end of the first century (Holmes 2007:337–8). The *Didascalia Apostolorum* (also "Teaching of the Apostles"), a manual primarily addressing Christian liturgical practices, is usually dated a hundred years later (early third century).

20 The Acts of the Apostles presents a number of speeches often identified as sermons (e.g. of Peter [2.14–36] and of Paul [13.16–41]). The canonical book of Hebrews also probably belongs in this category, along with 2 *Clement* (mid-second century?). Subsequent centuries would see an explosion of written homilies (e.g. by Origen in Caesarea Maritima [late second and third centuries CE], or by John Chrysostom in Syrian Antioch and Constantinople [fourth century CE]).

21 I would place the four canonical Gospels here, as well as the Acts of the Apostles. In the second and third centuries (and perhaps even in the first century) many other books were written that went by the name "Gospel" (e.g. the Gospel of Thomas, Gospel of Peter, Gospel of Truth, etc.) or "Acts" (e.g. Acts of Paul, Acts of Peter, etc.).

22 The early church wrote apocalypses (e.g. Revelation) and other types of visionary literature (e.g. *Shepherd of Hermas*), apologetic literature (e.g. *Diognetus*, the works of Justin Martyr), heresiological texts (e.g. Justin Martyr, Irenaeus), and others. Moreover, many non-Christian (esp. Jewish) texts were preserved and/or "Christianized" in the early church (e.g. *Wisdom of Solomon*, Testament of the Twelve Patriarchs, Josephus' *Antiquities of the Jews*, etc.). None of this, of course, even mentions the extensive production of biblical texts (canonical and deuterocanonical: Moses, the Prophets, the Writings, and the Apocrypha) and collections of testimonia.

23 Cited in Dewey 1995:51; see also Elman 1999:76–81; Horsley 2010:96 (Horsley differentiates between a "written text" and an "oral text," which refer, if I understand Horsley rightly, to different ways of accessing a scroll or codex—reading vs recitation from memory).

24 This question applies especially to the Gospels (and the three synoptic Gospels—Matthew, Mark, and Luke—in particular).

25 In the second edition (2005:85–6), the authors rewrite this paragraph. The changes begin at the sentence that begins, "But it is probable . . .": "At the same time, of course, much of the material was being passed on orally. But as time moved on, we can suspect that these early written fragments were combined with oral testimony to produce lengthier written sources and, finally, the canonical gospels. Source criticism is devoted to the investigation. . . ." Both explanations of the evolution from an oral (and fragmented written) stage of tradition to the canonical Gospels are inadequate in light of current theoretical and empirical research on interactions between oral and written expressions of tradition.

26 Chris Keith has argued that most historical Jesus research—viz.
that which employs the criteria of authenticity—has taken over this
aspect of form criticism and used it as a historical method (see Keith
2011a, b; 2012). For example, Ernst Fuchs based his lecture, "The
Quest of the Historical Jesus," on the historical-critical assumption
that "[i]t is possible to separate the material [in the Gospels] from its
framework" (Fuchs 1964:19, cited in Keith 2012:34–5).

Chapter 2

1 But not Joanna Dewey, who explicitly locates the written Gospel
of Mark "still on the oral side of the divide" (2008:73), or again,
"Whether composed in performance, by dictation, or in writing,
the Gospel of Mark was composed in an oral style and performed
orally. *The Gospel remains fundamentally on the oral side of the
oral/written divide*" (2008:86; my emphasis).

2 See the Wessex Parallel WebTexts Website, which has a useful
discussion as well as a helpful diagram illustrating *mouvance* (www.
southampton.ac.uk/~wpwt/mouvance/mouvance (accessed February
11, 2013)).

3 A third- or fourth-century CE apocryphal text, the *Narrative of
Joseph of Arimathea*, presents Jesus reading aloud a letter from the
cherubim who guard "the garden of paradise" (4.3; cited in Keith
2009:244). As far as I am aware, this is the first text to present Jesus
explicitly reading a written text other than Lk 4.16–21, although
other texts certainly present Jesus as a master of writing and of
written letters (e.g. *Infancy Gospel of Thomas*).

Chapter 3

1 Dibelius 1935; originally published as *Die Formgeschichte des
Evangeliums* (Tübingen: Mohr Siebeck, 1919).

2 Bultmann 1963; originally published as *Die Geschichte der
synoptischen Tradition* (Göttingen: Vandenhoeck & Ruprecht, 1921).

3 Schmidt's book, *Der Rahmen der Geschichte Jesu* (Berlin:
Trowitzsch & Sohn, 1919), was never translated into English.
Though he is nearly always mentioned alongside Dibelius and
Bultmann, Schmidt's influence is greatly eclipsed by the latter two,
especially among English-speaking scholars.

4 The very first sentence of Birger Gerhardsson's published dissertation mentions Dibelius and Bultmann (1961:9); Werner Kelber mentions Bultmann in the fifth sentence of his seminal *The Oral and the Written Gospel* (1983:1). Moreover, historians who have sought to take account of the findings of such studies also highlight form criticism's epochal significance for studying the oral Jesus tradition (e.g. Dunn 2003b:73–8).

5 A decade later Morna Hooker would level similarly devastating critiques against the propriety of employing form-critical methods for historical inquiry (see Hooker 1970, 1972). Hooker's critiques went largely unappreciated for over three decades and are only now beginning to receive the hearing they deserve (e.g. see the essays in Keith and Le Donne 2012).

6 Immediately after the quoted words (see 1961:328, n. 4), Gerhardsson refers back to his discussions of Rabbinic elementary teaching (1961:56–66) and Rabbinic transmission of the oral Torah (1961: 71–189). The book is peppered throughout with similar phrases; for example: In Acts 15 "Luke describes a doctrinal conflict between, on the one hand, a number of Jerusalem Christians, previously members of the Pharisaic party (presumably of bet Shammai), and, on the other, the Antiochene teachers Paul and Barnabas, of whom the former, at least, was a former Pharisee—and even a former pupil of bet Hillel. *We thus have every reason for comparing the course of this conflict with the corresponding phenomena in Rabbinic Judaism—at this early stage called Pharisaic Judaism*—or, to be more accurate, with rabbinic traditions of Jewish doctrinal controversies during the period of the Temple" (1961:249 [emphasis added; italics in the original have been removed]).

7 For a discussion of early Christian tradition in light of Hellenistic schools, see Alexander 2009.

8 Recently, Gerhardsson goes so far as to suggest that "in many pericopes even the words and the syllables have been counted" (2005:18)! A few minutes with any Gospel synopsis makes it difficult to think that any of our Evangelists worked with a conception of the Jesus tradition that counted and recounted precise words and syllables. Even fundamental teachings of Jesus (say, the Lord's Prayer, or the Greatest Commandment) evince considerable variation—in both words and syllables!—in their written manifestations and, certainly, also in their oral expressions.

9 Pieter Botha, a very sympathetic reader of Kelber's work, rightly notes, "Kelber tends to see orality and literacy as *alternatives* in his approach to the multifarious Jesus traditions" (1990:44; italics

in the original). Moreover, Kelber *does* use the term "great divide" (1983:203), and in such a way that clearly presupposes "something like a great gulf" (1983:203, citing Tödt 1965:232) between Q's orality and Mark's textuality, between the oral hermeneutics of the epistles and the textual hermeneutics of the Gospels. (I am thankful to Chris Keith [forthcoming] for this reference.)

10 Notice how Kelber has arrived at precisely the same conclusion as the form critics, namely: The pre-Gospel oral tradition is recoverable by dissolving the written Gospels into individual pericopes and neglecting its literary structure. "The stories we have studied exhibit full narrative self-sufficiency. . . . Eminently important as the literary comprehension of the gospel narratives is, we must not lose sight of the fact that many of their component parts represent modes of oral integrity. Our use of them in worship and instruction amply demonstrates their ability to function as self-contained oral units of communication. That they became building blocks for gospels can never be taken for granted, for they are anything but fragmented pieces in need of integration. . . . All are autonomous stories, and none are designed to build up a project of Markan proportions" (Kelber 1983:79).

11 This, I think, represents the greatest strength of Kelber's work, despite serious weaknesses at other places.

12 That is, Kelber's work provoked "a paradigmatic crisis" (Weeden 1979:156), and many scholars have risen to the challenge of reconceptualizing biblical scholarship in the wake of this crisis. To name only a few examples, see (1) the output of the SBL section, Bible in Ancient and Modern Media (BAMM), including two Semeia volumes (Silberman 1987; Dewey 1995), and (2) the reevaluation of memory and oral tradition among Jesus historians (e.g. Dunn 2003b; Bauckham 2006; Allison 2010). In addition, two unrelated volumes celebrate Kelber's work (Horsley et al. 2006; Thatcher 2008), and he has been an important voice in celebrating the work of other media critics (e.g. Birger Gerhardsson (see Kelber 2009) and Antoinette Clark Wire (see Kelber 2010)). Similar work rages among Hebrew Biblical and Judaic scholars. See the similar description of Kelber's legacy in Iverson 2009:77.

13 Similarly, see my critical appraisal of Davis 2008 in Rodríguez 2009:152–4.

14 Pieter Botha (1991:316) rightly avoids "testing for orality" in Mark's Gospel; instead, he recognizes that "the orality of Mark's gospel" must be argued on historical grounds rather than by strictly textual analyses.

15 See my critique of Dewey 1995 in Rodríguez 2009:166–70.

16 Achtemeier is emphatic here: "The important point for our purposes, however, is the fact that the oral environment was so pervasive that *no* writing occurred that was not vocalized. That is obvious in the case of dictation, but it was also true in the case of writing in one's own hand. . . . In the last analysis, dictation was the only means of writing; it was only a question of whether one dictated to another or to oneself" (1990:15; emphasis in the original).

17 Again, Achtemeier is emphatic: "Reading was therefore oral performance *whenever* it occurred and in whatever circumstances. Late antiquity knew nothing of the 'silent, solitary reader'" (1990:17; emphasis in the original).

18 See Gilliard 1993; Burnyeat 1997; Gavrilov 1997. Fusi 2003 56 provides a thorough discussion of the standard scholarly position and its weaknesses. David Cartlidge is spectacularly wrong, as is Joanna Dewey, who quotes him: "There is virtually no evidence to contradict the assertion that private, silent reading and writing simply did not exist in the period" (Cartlidge 1990:406, n. 37; quoted in Dewey 1992:46). See Johnson 2010:4–16 for a demonstration of (1) why this is the wrong answer to the question, Did (or Could) the ancients read aloud? and (2) why this is the wrong question to ask in the first place.

19 See Johnson 2010:7, n. 12, who calls Achtemeier's essay "a naive summary of the debate."

20 "Literacy can only be defined within a context. More than familiarity with reading and writing, literacy is about an ideologically laden social activity which is part of a cultural system" (Botha 1990:41). "[S]peaking broadly, scribal culture: culture familiar with writing but in essence still significantly, even predominantly, oral. In scribal culture reading is largely vocal and illiteracy the rule rather than the exception" (42).

21 Three years later, the problem persists. Botha writes, "In a cultural-anthropological sense, orality indicates a whole range of cognitive and social effects and values particular to an orally based communication technology" (1993b:415), but he never actually defines and describes these effects and values. See also Botha 2004. Moreover, Botha is not alone in this deficiency. In a lengthy section entitled, "What Do We Mean by an Oral Culture?" (Dunn 2005:89–101), James Dunn also never actually gets around to defining "oral culture," though he does provide some helpful characteristics of tradition (oral or written).

22 Botha explicitly opposes the form critics in his 1991 article: "Basic to Lord's approach is that the transmission of oral traditional material does not happen by memorisation of fixed stories. Recounting tradition is done by dynamic, thriving, and unique narrations by specific and talented individuals, not by nameless tradents. This is the opposite of the claims of *Formgeschichte*" (307).

23 Albert Lord made a similar proposal, describing the Gospels as "three oral traditional variants of the same narrative and non-narrative materials" and finding in them features that are "characteristic of oral traditional composition" (see Lord 1978; 90 cited).

24 Contrast Goodacre 2012:140–2. Goodacre focuses narrowly on the literacy of the NT authors and marginalizes the effect or significance of widespread illiteracy in the culture more broadly. "In early Christianity, there were many poor illiterates, but the literate elite were those who had command over the traditional material. Therefore *descriptions of the world in which early Christians moved as an 'oral culture' or of their mind-set as an 'oral mentality' are unhelpful*" (2012:141; emphasis added). Goodacre cites my judgment that the concepts of "oral mentality" and "oral culture" are unhelpful (Rodríguez 2009:157, cited by Goodacre 2012:141, n. 46), but he too quickly assumes that we can easily and naturally equate the NT authors' ability to read and/or to write with modern conceptions of literacy.

25 *P.Oxy.* 33.2673. For a discussion of this document, and in particular the surprising phenomenon of a lector who "does not know letters," see Choat and Yuen-Collingridge 2009.

26 Recall Gerhardsson's emphasis and consistent focus on the *transmission* of the oral Jesus tradition, which we discussed above (e.g. see Gerhardsson 2005).

27 Bailey describes the totally flexible material as "the telling of jokes, the reporting of casual news of the day, the reciting of tragedies in nearby villages and (in the case of inter-communal violence) atrocity stories" (1995:8). Earlier Bailey had said that one of his above-mentioned types of tradition falls into category of total flexibility, and the only type he has not placed into the no- and some-flexibility categories is "story riddles" (7). Are "story riddles" the same as/similar to jokes, casual news, and accounts of tragedies/atrocities?

28 Theodore Weeden (2009), in contrast, writes a detailed and unrelenting critique of Bailey's model. Though some of Weeden's criticisms are warranted, a number of them assume a narrowly literal reading of Bailey's anecdotal evidence. However, Weeden's entire essay exhibits a curious (ethnocentric? elitist?) disdain

for concrete empirical evidence in favor of abstract theoretical argumentation. Similarly, see Dunn 2009:48.

29 Of the eight uses of "authentic" or "authenticity" in Bailey 1995a, seven are used in the sense of "stability." Moreover, Bailey *never* (!) uses "authenticity" in the sense of "actuality."

30 See Wright 1996:133–6; Dunn 2003b:205–10, *passim*; 2005:45–6, 79–125.

31 For example, see Mournet 2005:187–91, 192–3, who follows Dunn in employing Bailey's model of informal controlled tradition to the Gospels.

32 Horsley provides only a one paragraph discussion of the then-nascent media criticism, with references to Achtemeier, Dewey, and Kelber. However, when he identifies potential paths of future research (1994:1144–5), Horsley does not explicitly mention media critical (or orality) studies. He focused narrowly on the *political* (rather than media) context of the NT texts, and his only other reference to Kelber (1994:1149) has nothing to do with issues of media.

33 See the discussion in the next chapter for the difference between the Ong/Havelock approach to "orality" and Foley's approach to "Immanent Art."

34 For a discussion of this passage and its claims for Jesus' literacy, see Keith 2010.

35 For a more technical and systematic survey of "the problem of oral tradition" among NT scholarship, see Mournet 2005:54–99. James Dunn (2003b:192–210) also provides a helpful discussion.

Chapter 4

1 Pieter Botha (1991), who advocates applying the Oral-Formulaic Theory to the Gospel of Mark, is not unaware of this problem and recognizes the generic and historical differences between the Gospels and the texts that Lord (and his teacher, Milman Parry) studied.

2 Craig Blomberg provides a list of six forms commonly adduced by form critics: (1) individual logia, or sayings, (2) pronouncement stories, (3) parables, (4) speeches, (5) miracle stories, and (6) other historical narratives ("Form Criticism," *DJG* 243–4). See also Figure 2.10 ("Form-Critical Categories") in Strauss 2007:56.

3 See E. P. Sanders's published doctoral dissertation (1969) for a devastating critique of this pillar of form-critical NT scholarship

(also, see Mournet 2005; Goodacre 2012:148–50). For the description of pre-Gospel oral transmission as obedient to "laws" of transmission, see Taylor 1933:26–7; Dibelius 1935:7–8. Despite Sanders's trenchant critique, the view of the law-governed evolution of tradition is still alive and well, especially in some scholars' attempts to reconstruct tradition histories.

4 See, for example, Davis 2008; Young 2011:81–97.

5 See also my discussion, later in the current chapter, of Egbert Bakker's "conceptual" sense of the adjective *oral*.

6 In the place where we would have expected Stephen Young to reproduce Ong's eighth psychodynamic (homeostatic), Young offers a different characteristic: "socially identified" (2011:91–6). Young fills out Ong's discussion of homeostasis with a brief discussion of the recent rise of social memory research in NT scholarship, but he does so from the starting point of homeostasis: "Not all oral traditions are preserved, but only those that remain socially relevant and acceptable. Some traditions that become socially obsolete are simply lost, while others are reinterpreted to continue to function in light of present realities" (2011:91–2, citing Ong 1982:46–9). Young rightly recognizes, "[t]he constant interplay between memory and present relevance in the performance of tradition continually generates ongoing syntheses, containing both past and present, *without either one canceling out the other*" (2011:92; emphasis added). However, he does not seem to recognize that this insight, which he discusses at some length (2011:93–6), fundamentally contradicts the idea of memory's (or orality's) homeostasis.

7 We will discuss this characteristic in detail, below, in conjunction with the work of James Dunn and Terence Mournet. Young offers a striking formulation: "[P]rovisionally stated, without stability, it would not be 'tradition,' without variability, it would not be 'oral'" (2011:87). This formulation is unhelpful, and Young immediately walks away from it in a footnote: "These statements are provisional because . . . the variability of oral tradition is not only associated with its orality, but also with its identity as tradition: tradition must be variable in order to remain viable or relevant" (2011:87, n. 67).

8 "The preservation of the integrity of traditions in an oral context depends on the ability of traditionists to accurately recall them. The latter requires a balance between both (a) *remembering* and (b) *memorizing* in a traditionist's preparation" (Young 2011:89).

9 See my discussion in Rodríguez 2009.

10 David Carr (2005) explains chiasms as an aid for memory rather than a feature of oral communication. This mnemonic explanation is much better, I think, than Dewey's media-critical explanation for chiasms.

11 At this very early stage in her career Dewey relies exclusively on Charles Lohr's essay, "Oral Techniques in the Gospel of Matthew" (1961). She offers no indications that she has read Eric Havelock or Albert Lord (esp. Lord 1978).

12 Note her conclusion: "There seems no reason on literary grounds to suppose that Mark 2:1–3:6 is not markan [*sic*]. . . . A fondness for stressing contrast is characteristic of markan [*sic*] style and literary technique. . . . Since both frames and interpositions (including intercalations and insertions) are markan [*sic*] literary devices, the redactor would seem to be Mark" (1980:184, 185).

13 We can see a shift, similar to what we saw for Dewey's approach to inclusio between 1980 and 1989, in her treatment of parataxis and Mark's structuring techniques in general: "Mark unquestionably has a fondness for certain literary devices. Nonetheless such devices belong to *a pool of techniques generally available to all narrators—whether of oral or written material.* And it can be as problematic to determine the origin of any specific instance of a literary device as it is to determine if any given saying in the gospels contains the *ipsissima verba* of Jesus. The same problems exist that exist in the use of style as an indicator of Mark's active redaction of a text: the use of the historic present and καί parataxis are unquestionably markan [*sic*] stylistic characteristics, yet both are also characteristics of oral literature" (1980:8; emphasis added).

14 The five characteristic features are (1) oral performance is not like reading a literary text, (2) oral tradition is essentially communal in character, (3) the oral community includes one or more individuals who are primarily responsible for maintaining and performing the community's tradition, (4) oral tradition subverts the concept of a singular "original version," and (5) oral tradition is characteristically a combination of stability and variability (Dunn 2005:93–9). Note that points (1) and (3) are not, technically, characteristics of oral tradition. Points (2), (4), and (5) do apply to oral tradition, but they also apply, of course, to written tradition (e.g. see Parker 1997 for a seminal discussion of the inherent flexibility of manuscript tradition [see Dunn's point (5)] and the problematic notion of "*the* original text" among text critics [see Dunn's point (4)]).

15 Walter Ong offers a wonderful and helpful analogy of trying to describe a horse to people who are only familiar with automobiles and the unfortunate limitations of using automobile categories to explain what a horse is (Ong 1982:12–13, cited by Dunn 2005:89–90). Ong and those who follow him reject referring to "oral texts," which they say is as distorting as referring to horses as "wheelless automobiles." Nevertheless, the term is firmly established among scholars of oral tradition from across the Humanities, and I use it as a helpful way to refer to the verbal message of an oral performance.

16 See Parker 1997:31–48; the text of all three codices is laid out in parallel columns, with synoptic notations, on 34–5.

17 "[T]he very process of transmitting texts was itself a radically conservative process. These scribes understood that they were conserving rather than creating tradition" (Ehrman 1993:58) Similarly, "we must rest content knowing that getting back to the earliest attainable version is the best we can do, whether or not we have reached back to the 'original' text. This oldest form of the text is no doubt closely (*very* closely) related to what the author originally wrote, and so it is the basis for our interpretation of his teaching" (Ehrman 2005:62; italics in the original). I am grateful to my colleague, Carl Bridges, for bringing this quote to my attention.

18 See Ong 1982:36–57, discussed in Young 2011:81–97.

19 Young does not cite Bakker 2005. Instead, he cites some of Bakker's older works (especially 1997, 1999). With respect to the current question ("oral" as a distinctive conceptualization of language and discourse), Bakker's earlier work is largely taken up and reproduced in *Pointing at the Past*.

20 Bakker originally offered a graphic depiction with only the first two continua (1999:31). Since Young only interacts with his older work, he only offers this truncated presentation of Bakker's theoretical perspective (see Young 2011:71).

21 I have taken (or in one case, derived) the terms "subordinative," "analytic," and "innovative" from Ong's contrast between the psychodynamics of orality versus chirographic thought and expression (see Ong 1982:37, 38, 41).

22 Again, the terms "additive," "aggregative," and "traditionalist" come from Ong's list of orality's psychodynamics (see the previous note).

23 I would also offer another criticism of Bakker's three-continua model: There is no necessary connection between the first continuum (oral ⟨—⟩ literate) and the other two. However, since I

am dismissing the first continuum completely, there is no need to address the issue whether it is necessarily related to the other two.

24 In addition, as I said in the previous paragraph, whether oral language can exhibit the features media critics ascribe to "literate" discourse or thought is somewhat more controversial, but it hardly matters here.

25 Young does not explain why the "replacement" of spoken phonemes with written graphemes automatically results in the transformation of the text's characteristics. Worse, he does not explain why spoken phonemes are *replaced* by written graphemes. Instead, written and spoken signs work together as vehicles of signification.

26 See the helpful appraisal of the concept *orality*—including both its advantageous and the unhelpful consequences—in Finnegan 1990.

27 Notice Dunn's significant and completely appropriate stipulation, noted above, that the interplay of stability and variability is "not . . . distinctively" characteristic of oral tradition. In other words, oral tradition may exhibit both stability and variability (though it does not always do so, as Dunn knows full well; see 2003b:206–7), but this does not differentiate oral tradition from written tradition. Anyone who has spent five minutes reading about NT textual criticism knows full well that written tradition frequently exhibits these same characteristics. But why, then, should we attribute this interplay to the tradition's *medium*?

28 Again, Aune provides a helpful corrective: "While it is impossible to disprove that composition techniques have a proximate oral origin, neither is it possible to prove that they actually do. The reason is that there is a revolving door between oral and written composition. *Virtually all of the compositional techniques used originally in oral composition made a seamless transition into the stylistics of written composition*" (2009:74; emphasis added).

29 Careful readers may have spotted my very literate, print-based use of inclusio to emphasize this conclusion.

30 Mournet explains that the term "verbal art" comes from William Bascom, who proposed the term "in an attempt to describe the fluid character of oral performance" (2005:14, citing Bascom 1955).

31 Bultmann described the Gospels as "unliterary" and so finds that "one of the chief differences between oral and written traditions is lacking" (1963:6), though he does not explain what that difference is. E. P. Sanders accepted the presumption that "there would have been little difference between written and oral tradition during the first century" (1969:7).

32 This is a crucial point. When Foley refers to "inherent" versus "conferred" meaning, for example, he is not saying that we can place a text (whether oral or written) within one category or the other. Rather, any work of verbal art will be subject to both inherent and conferred dynamics of meaning though the influence of those dynamics will vary from text to text.

33 The modern legal concept of copyright explicitly codifies the rights and responsibilities of the creative genius behind certain classes of works. In contrast, we refer to certain works as belonging to the "public domain," a designation that may imply that those works are "traditional" in the sense we are discussing or may simply indicate that the rights and responsibilities afforded by copyright status have lapsed.

34 "In classical Gr[eek] of the early period *kyrios* was not used as a divine title. Although the term was applied to the gods . . . the Gr[eek] of this period did not understand his position as that of a slave (*doulos*), dependent on a god. Nor did he feel himself in any way personally responsible to the gods. Only in so far as the gods ruled over particular individual spheres in the world could they be called *kyrioi*" (*NIDNTT* 2.510).

35 "And his [= John's] disciples reported to John about all of these things. And John summoned two of his disciples and sent them to the Lord [*pros ton kyrion*], asking, 'Are you the one who is coming, or should we expect someone else?'" (Lk. 7.18–19).

36 The parallel passage in Matthew says simply that John sent his disciples "to him" [*autō*], but earlier Matthew referred to "the messiah's deeds" [*to erga tou Christou*] (Mt. 11.2–3).

37 Foley comments on the unequal distribution of talent among traditional performers. "The lesser of them use the traditional inheritance with limited success; the more dexterous will both command its inherent possibilities with greater precision and fidelity to the tradition *and make more impact by the individual conferral of meaning*" (1991:8–9; emphasis added). See also Botha 1991:307.

38 Examples of a source-critical conception of oral tradition are common among media critics. For example: "[T]he closer a text is placed to the [oral] extreme of the continua, the more it must be studied not as a written composition but as *the spoken word that preceded its transcription*" (Young 2011:72; emphasis added).

39 Media critics almost always make this point (including the present volume). As another example: "The living voice, however, is a fleeting voice. Since no oral performances of the Gospels or the

other writings of the New Testament remain, what can we know
about the way they were performed?" (Shiner 2009:50–1). We do
have to be careful, however. For example, Shiner is alluding to the
famous comment from Papias, the early-second-century bishop
of Hierapolis (in modern-day Turkey): "I did not suppose that
information from books would help me so much as the word of a
living and surviving voice" (Eusebius, *Hist. eccl.* 3.39.1–4, quoted
in Shiner 2009:50). The word translated "surviving" is *menousēs*,
which literally means "abiding" or "enduring" (BDAG, *s.v.*). Notice,
then, that despite our own emphasis on the oral word's evanescence
("the living voice . . . is a fleeting voice"), Papias portrays the living
voice as "enduring," a quality he explicitly contrasts with the
impermanence of the written record ("information from books").

40 The second-century CE pagan critic of Christianity, Celsus, appears
to have read the Gospel of Matthew and was familiar with various
noncanonical Christian texts (Hoffmann 1987).

41 Another problem plagues readers who cannot rely on their
experiences with the communal performance of the Markan
tradition. That is, even when readers think they have identified a
link running between the text and the tradition, they cannot really
be sure that traditional audiences would have identified that same
specific link. For example, does Mark's explicit mention of "the
green grass" (*tō chlōrō chortō*) in 6.39 relate to the traditional
obligation of a shepherd to lead his sheep to green pastures (see
Ps. 23.2; Mk 6.34, cited by France 2002:266–7)? Or does it
implicitly refer to the blossoming desert, a signal of the dawn of
the messianic age (see Ezek. 34.26–9; Isa. 51.3, cited by Mauser
1963:136–7; Marcus 1992:24)? Or is it simply a detail that does not
merit any special consideration (see Yarbro Collins 2007:324–5,
who does not comment on the traditional significance of "the green
grass" [though see 320, 322])? For a helpful introduction to the
question of identifying intertextual allusions, see Hays 1989:25–32;
Allison 2000:1–24.

42 The quotation marks should not give the impression that, two years
later, I remember this scholar's exact words.

43 See Johnson 2010:4–9.

44 See Shiner 2003, 2009. In his chapter on "Types of Oral
Performance" (2003:37–56), Shiner discusses both private readings
(37–9) and public readings (39–40), in addition to other, more
intuitive examples of [oral] performance. See also Botha 2005.

45 Chris Keith, for example, follows Jan Assmann: "*the* categorical
distinction between oral tradition and written tradition is that

writing does not demand the 'copresence' of the transmitter of the tradition and the audience that ritual and festival require" (forthcoming; emphasis in the original). Written tradition may not *demand* the "copresence" of transmitter and audience. Nevertheless, NT media critics need to consider whether or not a manuscript *usually* involved their copresence. In my view, especially given the low distribution of literacy skills in the first-century CE, even written manuscripts functioned in contexts similar to (or even exactly the same as) "ritual and festival."

46 Foley addresses these three aspects in his discussion of actually oral verbal art (see 1995a:47–56) and then again in his discussion of the "transformation(s)" from oral performance to an oral-derived text (see 1995a:78–95).

47 Notice that Foley (1995a:80) also puts the word "place" within quotation marks.

48 For a suggestive (rather than comprehensive) discussion of the beginnings of the four canonical Gospels and their rhetorical strategies for summoning their appropriate performance arenas, see Rodríguez 2010:107–9.

49 See our discussion, above, of Foley's two binary tensions (conferred vs inherent meaning; denotative vs connotative meaning).

50 So a Tibetan paper-singer may require "a text," a piece of paper or even a piece of newsprint, to tell the tales of King Gesar, but he does not "read" the text because he *cannot* read it. He is illiterate. His verbal art is still properly classified as Oral Performance, but given that "the story of King Gesar appears in his mind" when he fixates on the paper, we have moved in the direction of Voiced Texts, even if only slightly. See Foley 2002:1–3, *passim* (3 quoted).

51 Whenever I use the phrase "Oral Performance" to refer to this type of verbal art, I will capitalize the phrase to distinguish this usage from "oral performance" (lowercase), the oral presentation of tradition without any implication of the absence or presence of written texts. See Foley 2002:40–3.

52 See Foley 2002:43–5.

53 See Shiner 2003 for a suggestive reconstruction of how the Gospel of Mark might have functioned as a script enabling oral performance.

54 See Foley 2002:45–50.

55 Foley refers to "a sensible agnosticism" and argues that a model that forces us to acknowledge our ignorance of some things actually enhances our knowledge of other things. "If we attempt to force too

much order on such diversity, if we try to impose too much from the outside by making assertions we can't substantiate, any system of media dynamics will be compromised. At that point it will be only too easy to collapse all verbal art back into our default category of text-bound literature" (2002:47).

56 Bauckham 1997 argues that the Gospel of John was written for an audience that was already familiar with the Gospel of Mark (though see North 2003 for a critical response). Goodacre 2012 argues that the *Gospel of Thomas* was familiar with the synoptic Gospels, especially Matthew and Luke.

Chapter 5

1 BDAG, *s.v.*

2 Similarly: "it is not surprising that both Matt. 4:1 and Luke 4:1 change [*ekballō*] to 'led' (ἤγετο; *ēgeto*) or a related root of 'led' (ἀνήχθη, *anēchthē*)" (Stein 2008:63). Unlike Evans, however, Stein offers no explanation for Mark's use of *ekballō*.

3 In Mt. 9.38 Jesus instructs the disciples, "Pray, therefore, of the lord of the harvest, that he would cast out [*ekbalē*] workers into his harvest" (see also Mt. 9.25; 12.20, 35; 13.52). The parallel passage in Lk. 10.2 is identical, with only the slightest difference in word order. (For a similar use of *ekballō* in Luke, see Lk. 10.35.) This makes Mt. 9.38‖Lk. 10.2 a Q passage. If Evans' explanation of Matthew's and Luke's redaction of Mk 1.12 is right, why have neither of our evangelists similarly redacted Q 10.2?

4 Mark uses *ekballō* 16 times (excluding 16.9, 17), with ten of those 16 (including 3.23) referring to exorcisms. We should note that, given the inappropriateness of the English word *exorcise* for contexts such as Mk 5.40 ("Then he sent [*ekbalōn*; lit. 'cast'] all of them out"), we should recognize significant semantic differences between the English *to exorcise* (and the exorcistic overtones intended in *to cast out*) and *ekballō*. Louw and Nida list *ekballō* four times under semantic domain no. 15 ("Linear Movement") and once under domain no. 13 ("Be, Become, Exist, Happen"), in addition to one under domain no. 53 ("Religious Activities"); see L&N 2.76.

5 Edwards 2002:23 mentions Genesis and Hosea (and John). Any resonance with Genesis is fainter by virtue of the prepositional phrase, "*In* the beginning . . ." (Gen. 1.1), but I would not discount

that Mark may also activate the larger creation tradition as the reference to which his own account points.

6 Scholars also recognize a close verbal correspondence between Mk 1.2 and Exo. 23.20: "And **behold, I am sending my messenger before you,** so that he will guard you on the way and you will enter the land which I prepared for you" (LXX; words in **bold typeface** correspond exactly between the Greek of Mk 1.2 and Exo. 23.20; underlined words indicate significant but not identical verbal correspondences between the two texts).

7 I appreciate that many readers will be uncomfortable referring to Mk 1.2 as an "error." For this reason, I have used quotation marks to acknowledge that we can explain this verse in ways other than saying that Mark made a mistake. Nevertheless, even those of us with a "high view of Scripture" need to be able to recognize that, in any other circumstance, if someone claims to quote one author and instead quotes another, we usually and normally call that an "error" or a "mistake."

8 For example, "And it shall come to pass, whenever all these words come upon you—the blessing as well as the curse which I have set before you—and you will receive them into your heart among all the nations, wherever the Lord scatters you, and you will return to the Lord your Go and obey his voice in all these words, as much as I am commanding you today, with all your heart and with all your should, and the Lord will heal your sins and have mercy upon you, and again he will gather you from all the nations, to whom the Lord scattered you" (Deut. 30.1–3 LXX).

9 Nevertheless, throughout his commentary proper Edwards regularly notes the biblical and traditional resonances of Mark's narrative, though he has not allowed those resonances to soften his (over) confidence that "[t]here can be little doubt that Mark wrote for Gentile readers, and Roman Gentiles in particular" (2002:10).

10 Commentators note that *ekballei* in 1.12 is the first occurrence of "the historical present" in Mark. This strange (to us) stylistic feature of Mark—which Matthew mutes considerably and Luke nearly silences—may provide one of the signals marking the switch to the "value-added," dedicated idiom of the tradition (similarly, see Foley 2002:15–16). Mark uses the historical present 151 times, significantly more than Matthew (78) and Luke (six), "even though each is approximately 70 percent larger than Mark" (Stein 2008:62–3).

11 Compare *ekballō* in Genesis, which describes Adam's and Cain's expulsion from God's presence (3.24; 4.14, respectively), and

Sarah's insistence that Abraham dismiss "this slave girl and her son" (21.10). Leviticus, not unlike Gen. 21.10, uses *ekballō* three times (of six) to refer to a divorced woman (NETS: "a woman rejected by her husband"; Lev. 21.7, 14; 22.13), as does Num. 30.10. Leviticus uses *ekballō* once in a sacrificial context (Lev. 1.16) and once in a purity context (Lev. 14.40). Other than these nine, three of *ekballō*'s appearances in the Pentateuch parallel the second half of Exodus (see Num. 21.32; Deut. 11.23; 33.27), and three times it refers to an expulsion curse against Israel, whether Balaam's unutterable curse (Num. 22.6, 11) or YHWH's curse for violation of the covenant (Deut. 29.27).

12   In Exod. 10.11, Pharoah's attendants drive Moses out of Pharoah's presence. I take this as an example of the larger theme of the Israelites' expulsion out of Egypt. The other four uses occur at Exod. 6.1; 11.1; 12.33, and 12.39.

13   See Exod. 23.18, 28–31 (4x); 33.2; 34.11, and 34.24.

14   For example, Deut. 8.2: "And you shall remember the entire way, on which the Lord your God led you in the wilderness, so that he would afflict you and test you (*ekpeirasē se*), and the things that are in your heart might be discerned, whether or not you would keep his commandments" (LXX).

15   I agree with Caneday, that "it appears likely that it is Israel's wilderness testing that serves as the dominant reference for Mark" (1999:30).

16   Mt. 4.4‖Lk. 4.4 cite Deut. 8.3; Mt. 4.7‖Lk 4.12 cite Deut. 6.16; Mt. 4.10‖Lk. 4.8 cite Deut. 6.13.

17   The majority of NT scholars accept some version of the Two- (or Four-)Source Theory, which affirms (1) Markan priority and (2) Matthew's and Luke's independent use of Q; see Strauss 2007:48–53.

18   A growing minority of NT scholars, led especially by Mark Goodacre, accept the Farrer Theory, which affirms (1) Markan priority and (2) Luke's use of both Mark and Matthew; see Goodacre 2002.

19   For example, the *gradatio* in Jn 1.1–2 ("In the beginning was the *logos*, and the *logos* was with God"), which "can easily be accounted for as an expansion of the formal rhetorical pattern found in the first verse of Genesis: 'In the beginning God created the heaven and the *earth*, and the *earth* was without form and void'" (Boyarin 2004:96).

20 The present form of the verb "I am" (*eimi*) in Mk 1.7 is the same word as Jn 1.15's "he was" (*ēn*), but the words are not parallel. In Mark, *eimi* is in the present tense and refers to John the Baptist; in the Fourth Gospel, *ēn* is in the imperfect tense and refers to the incarnated Word (v. 14).

21 Surprisingly, despite his recognition that the *logos* of God is a creative force (or entity) in the Johannine Prologue, O'Grady emphasizes the revelatory functions of the *logos* in order to heighten the links between the Prologue in John 1 and the prayer in John 17: "Jesus is the Word of God, and thus when he speaks, he reveals God. . . . In chapter 17, the Word speaks and explains the relationship between Jesus and God the Father and the relationship between the disciples and God through Jesus" (2007:223, 224). Culpepper provides a more precise perspective. The Word is God's creative force (e.g. 1983:57), but "The prologue links *logos*, life, and light so powerfully that the cluster dominates the symbolic system of the entire narrative. . . . Light is not only the revelation of the *logos*; it reveals the nature of all who come in contact with it, and the judgment upon each person is determined by his or her response to it. Light shines in darkness. It reveals. It also exposes" (1983:190, 191). In other words, the revelatory symbol in the Prologue is *light*, the object of the creative function of the *logos*.

22 That is, even if Paul did not write the so-called deutero-Pauline epistles (say, Colossians), the ascription in Col. 1.1 ("Paul, an apostle of Christ Jesus through the will of God, and Timothy the brother") nevertheless summons the Pauline *persona* as the rhetorical, implied author whose authority vouchsafes the contents and motivates the ethical instructions contained in the epistle to the Colossians. On the author side of the communications model, the Petrine address in 1 Pet. 1.1 ("To those who are chosen, strangers of the Diaspora residing in Pontus, Galatia, Cappadocia, Asia, and Bithynia") summons the Israelite/Judean Diaspora *persona* as the rhetorical implied readership despite being addressed to actual gentile Christians (see 1 Pet. 1.14, 18; 4.3; *passim*). In other words, even if Paul did not write Colossians and Peter (or the Petrine author) did not envision a Jewish audience, these ascriptions nevertheless play an important role in how the texts portray their composition and expect to be received.

23 With respect to Galatians (which does not explicitly identify its letter carrier), Botha says, "In view of typical practice, the fact that so much was invested in the letter, and the import attached to the letter, one must reckon with the letter as having been prepared for

a careful performance, and that *eventually the letter was delivered like a proper speech*" (1992:24; emphasis added).

24 Or again, "Voiced Texts live only in, and solely for, oral performance . . . and their audience knows them only as oral poems" (Foley 2002:45).

25 This is a dramatic simplification. For example, see Metzger and Ehrman 2005:272–3 for a brief discussion of the difficulties in referring to "the original text of the Pauline epistles." However, this simplification serves a legitimate point: the act of writing is much more significant as a moment of origination for the NT epistles than it is for the narrative Gospels.

26 The classic definition of "rhetorical situation" comes from Lloyd Bitzer: "Rhetorical situation may be defined as a complex of persons, events, objects, and relations presenting an actual or potential exigence which can be completely or partially removed if discourse, introduced into the situation, can so constrain human decision or action as to bring about the significant modification of the exigence" (1968:6).

27 For morphological approaches to oral tradition in Paul's letters, see Harvey 1998 and Davis 1999. For analyses of (oral) Jesus tradition in Paul, see Holtz 1991; Keightley 2005; and Aune 2009. A third area of inquiry concerns performance-critical readings of Paul, which explore how the actual oral performance of a Pauline letter affect its social function and interpretation (e.g. A. Dewey 1995; Ward 1995). Akio Ito's essay (2006) deals directly with our text (Rom. 10.5–13) and appeals to "orality and literacy" [*sic*] to explain the text. However, his discussion falters in two of its first steps: (1) he assumes that "some sort of contrast between 'the righteousness from the Torah' and 'the righteousness from faith'" (2006:236) equates to an antithesis between Torah and gospel or even grace and works; (2) he works with an unnuanced and too-sharp distinction between oral and written communication (2006:243–6). Ito denies a "simple opposition between orality and literacy" in the world of the NT, and he offers the caveat that "[p]robably we should think in terms of a nuanced tension between orality and literacy, not a simple opposition" (244). Even so, he never explains the precise mechanics of the tension he assumes characterizes the relation between speaking and writing.

28 Kelber focuses particularly on the opposition of "spirit" (*pneuma*) and "letter" (*gramma*) in 2 Corinthians 3. I am applying Kelber's reading of 2 Corinthians 3 to Romans 10. Kelber's approach to the problem of Paul's view of the Mosaic Law is clearly evident in the

following: "Paul's concern, we observed, is the grammatological nature of the Law. The principal antithesis is not between Spirit versus works, but between Spirit versus the Written. Paul's objection is not to the *nomos* as a legal authority, but rather to the objectification of the Law as *gramma*" (1983:158). I doubt that Kelber has accurately read the media dynamics of 2 Corinthians 3; in the present discussion I will show that Kelber's approach certainly does not apply to Romans 10 (*pace* Ito 2006).

29   See Wallace 1996:203–4, who translates Rom. 10.5 as an "accusative of respect or (general) reference"; similarly, see BDF §160 (which does not refer to Rom. 10.5). I have added the word "revealed" here and in v. 6 on the basis of this passage's thematic and lexical similarity to Rom. 3.21–2, where Paul talks about the righteousness of God "being revealed" (*pephanerōtai*) apart from Torah.

30   Arthur Dewey highlights Paul's personification of "righteousness" (*dikaiosynē*): "Most crucial for our investigation is that Paul personifies *Dikaiosune* [*sic*] . . . Here Paul gives a new voice (*Dikaiosune* [*sic*]) to the tradition, which transforms the understanding of the written tradition" (1995:115, 116). While I will disagree radically with the conclusions Dewey draws from Romans 10, he is right to recognize that Paul gives voice to personified righteousness—*Dikaiosynē*—who now stands revealed by Christ's faithfulness (*pistis Christou*).

31   See Dunn 1988:596–8 and Jewett 2007:619–20 for two very different readings of this verse. See also the important (but now somewhat dated) discussion in Badenas 1985.

32   The participle, "the one who reads" (*ho anaginōskōn*) in Rev. 1.3 is the only instance of the verb "to read" (*anaginōskein*) in Revelation.

33   We should, however, recognize limits to what could or should be written in particular contexts. When John hears the mighty angel roaring like a lion and the seven thunders speaking and he prepares to write down what he hears, a heavenly voice stops him: "Seal up the things that the seven thunders said, and do not write them" (Rev. 10.3–4; v. 4 quoted).

34   Stefanović (1996:119–45) provides a lengthy discussion of the word *biblion* and, specifically, the seven-sealed *biblion* described in Revelation 5. "In Revelation the word βιβλίον occurs twenty-three times and is applied in five different senses: (1) The βιβλίον of prophecy, equated with Revelation itself, which was sent to the Christian communities in Asia (1:11; 22:7, 9, 18–19) and was not

supposed to be sealed (22:10); (2) the βιβλίον sealed with seven seals (chap. 5); (3) the βιβλαρίδιον ('the little book') which John had to eat (chap. 10); (4) τὸ βιβλίον τῆς ζωῆς, the book of life (13:8; 17:8; 20:12; 21:27); and (5) τὰ βιβλία (plural) which are related to the final judgment (20:12)" (1996:120).

35 I will argue below that the verbs "consume" and "eat" (*katesthiō* and *esthiō*, respectively) in 10.9–10 connote the act of reading.

36 I have counted the seven "openings" of the seven seals in Revelation 6, 8.1 as a single event, since they all refer to the singular opening of the one scroll described in Revelation 5.

37 I have made a similar argument in relation to Lk. 4.16–21; see Rodríguez 2010:158–63.

38 Hurtado 1985 argues that Revelation 4 and 5 are a tightly linked unit, "an integrally ordered heavenly vision that is significantly influenced by the writer's Christian faith," and "a notable mutation on the pattern of heavenly visions in the Jewish apocalyptic background" (1985:118).

39 According to Stefanović, interpretations of Revelation 5 have focused on one of two issues: the contents of the scroll or the possible background for the enthronement scene (1996:114–17). We are ignoring completely the first issue and are only tangentially concerned with the second. Stefanović's third chapter, "Background and Meaning of the Sealed BIBΛION" (1996:228–313) focuses explicitly on the meaning of the sealed scroll in the enthronement scene of Revelation 4–5.

40 I have also searched for the synonyms *biblos* and *biblaridion*. In order to avoid having to reproduce all three words throughout the discussion that follows, any general statements about *biblion* will also stand true for *biblos* and *biblaridion* unless otherwise noted.

41 For example, on two occasions the *biblion* is equivalent to a letter (*epistolē*; see 2 Kgs 5.5–7; 10.6–7 LXX). In 2 Kings 22–3||2 Chronicles 34–5 (total of 13 references), the *biblion* refers to the Book of the Covenant that was found in the Temple and sparked Josiah's Reform. In 2 Kgs 20.12, the king of Babylon sends gifts of scrolls (*biblia*) and manna to the sick Hezekiah.

42 Stefanović 1996:229–34.

43 The Hebrew text reads *kissē'* ("throne"), which the LXX translates *thronos* 118 times. This is the only instance in which the LXX translates *kisse'* with *archē*.

44 The Hebrew text reads *mamlaktô* ("kingdom"), which the LXX translates *basileia* (or cognate) 99 times. The LXX translates

mamlaktô with *archē* five times. Although the Greek phrases in v. 18 and in v. 20 are identical (*epi tēs archēs autou*; lit. "upon his power/beginning"), the referent in v. 18 is clearly the king's throne, while the referent in v. 20 is less specific.

45 Similarly, see Stefanović's discussion of near eastern (esp. Hittite) covenant-treaty forms and those forms' relevance for Israelite coronation ritual (1996:234–63).

46 We could also contrast the lamb with the revelatory angel in Rev. 19.10 and 22.9. When John falls at the angel's feet in order to worship him, the angel stops John, exclaiming, "No! Don't! I am a servant, like you and your brethren who have the testimony of Jesus" (19.10). The wording of Rev. 22.9 is exactly the same as 19.10 up until the description of John's brethren and the addition of a third comparison: "No! Don't! I am a servant, like you, your brethren the prophets, and all those who keep the words of this book."

47 In addition to royal decrees and edicts, legal documents were also sealed in order to prevent tampering and guarantee their authenticity. In the case of legal documents, the witnesses also added their seals onto the text (see Stefanović 1996:137–40).

48 Osborne nicely expresses the "close connection between the scroll visions of chapters 5 and 10": "the scroll that was opened progressively with the breaking of the seals in 6:1–8:1 now lies 'open' in the hand of this mighty angel" (see 2002:393–5; 393 quoted).

49 "The majority of scholars have assumed that [the 'little scroll' in Rev. 10] is a different scroll from that of Revelation 5 because John calls it a βιβλαρίδιον. However, this is probably not to be pressed (cf. ἀρνίον, θηρίον). The sealed scroll of Revelation 5 has been opened (Rev. 6–8) and is now given to John to digest. Thus it seems clear that Ezekiel's scroll is the main inspiration behind Revelation 5 and Revelation 10" (Moyise 1995:77). *Pace* Linton (1993:205–6): "Once the seventh seal is opened, this scroll is never mentioned again. However, several other books are mentioned, including the little scroll of chapter 10, the book of life, books of the deeds of people, and the book of the prophecy that John wrote." Aune (1998:571) is ambivalent on the matter; first he lists six reasons for identifying the *biblion* of chapter 5 with the *biblaridion* of chapter 10, but then he offers three reasons against identifying them, which he describes as "weighty."

50 Although he does not focus on the question whether John utilizes a Greek or a Hebrew text of the Hebrew Bible (Old Testament),

Jan Fekkes finds that John generally engages the Hebrew textual tradition. "The verdict of R. H. Charles that the prophet invariably 'draws his materials directly form the Hebrew (or Aramaic) text' has been corroborated in a variety of subsequent studies, and my own analysis has yielded nothing to weaken this opinion. . . . There are occasions where John may be in touch with a Greek tradition (either directly or indirectly), and, likewise, a few examples which appear to reflect targumic and rabbinic traditions. But for the most part, it seems clear that John is working from a knowledge of the Hebrew text, and unless otherwise stated, this is the presupposition adopted in individual lexical comparisons" (Fekkes 1994:16–17, citing Charles 1920:lxvi). The Septuagint of Gen. 49.9–10 does not mention the scepter (*skēptron*) or the staff (*rhabdos*); instead, it mentions a ruler (*archōn*) and a leader (*hēgoumenos*). However, I am interpreting John's vision against the Hebrew *Vorlage* of Gen. 49.9–10.

51   According to Fekkes, John alludes specifically to Isa. 11.10 and not to Isa. 11.1 (1996:150). Such precision exceeds the dynamics of Revelation 5. When the elder points John's gaze to "the lion from the tribe of Judah, the shoot of David," John does not necessarily have any particular *text* in view but rather the *tradition* of the Davidic shoot, rising from the root of Jesse over the now-fallen forest of foreign powers, in order to reestablish the Lord's reign over the nations.

52   See Rev. 6.15; 15.3; 17.14; 19.16; 21.24.

53   See, for example, Bauckham 1993:179–85; Osborne 2002:252–4; Resseguie 2009:117–19. Aune rightly sees both royal and sacrificial significance in John's use of the lamb metaphor (1998:352, 368–73); this double significance is reinforced by the juxtaposition of the two images: a lion, but also a lamb.

54   Aune frequently mentions the "widely known story" within which the series of visions in Revelation make sense to John's audience.

55   Aune refers to "numerous reliefs from the period of the Roman empire that depict an emperor holding a scroll in his hand," and he concludes: "This scroll in the hands of various emperors apparently functions as a symbol of imperial power and authority" (1998:341). In the passages we have considered, however, the written text simultaneously inscribes the king's *authority over* the populace and his *submission to* God/the gods. The function of the seven-sealed scroll as an emblem of the lamb's authority in Revelation 5 operates in a strikingly different way.

56 See also my discussion of the distinctive conception of "reading" in Lk. 4.16–21 in Rodríguez 2010:158–63.

57 For general discussions of reading aloud in antiquity, see Achtemeier 1990; Gamble 1995:203–5; Mournet 2005:133–41; Hearon 2008:101–3; Young 2011:73, 78–9. Interestingly, none of these discussions specifically mentions Rev. 1.3. (Gamble discusses Rev. 1.3 in his analysis of the function and status of the *lector* in early Christianity, but he does not address this text's significance for discussions of reading aloud; see Gamble 1995:219). Contemporary culture provides certain analogues to this sense of "reading," as when an author offers a public reading in a bookstore, a lector reads a sacred text in the context of a worship service, or a volunteer reads a story to children in a library.

58 The second-person singular imperative *grapson* ("write") occurs 12 times throughout Revelation: nine times before the appearance of the scroll in Revelation 5 (see Rev. 1.11, 19; 2.1, 8, 12, 18; 3.1, 7, 14) and three times after John eats the open scroll in Revelation 10 (see Rev. 14.13; 19.9; 21.5). The curses in Rev. 22.18–19 protect the integrity of the contents of the book of Revelation and, if commentators are right, to equate the contents of Revelation with the scroll in chapters 5 and 10, of the seven-sealed scroll itself.

59 Heb. = *dabbēr*; Grk = *lalēson*.

60 Contrast Luke's portrayal of the Diaspora Jews in Berea (Acts 17.10–13), who "examined the scriptures" (v. 11) in order to verify the accuracy of Paul's message.

61 As such, NT media criticism transcends the literary-critical interest in "intertextuality," which focuses narrowly on the written text and its interaction with (or interference from) other written texts. With respect to intertextuality, Foley rightly observes, "[W]e can observe that the very etymology of that critical term denominates two or more formally bounded, complete items that interact—so that their separate contexts are more or less sharply defined, and the individual text maintains an absolute status uniquely its own. Even though the field of interpretation is enlarged and deepend, textual heuristics tacitly demands that we privilege the individual document above all else" (1995a:xi). Media-critical analyses of the NT aim at situating the texts holistically within their traditional contexts rather than merely reading them in relation to other individual written texts.

WORKS CITED

Achtemeier, Paul J. 1990. "*Omne Verbum Sonat*: The New Testament and the Oral Environment of Late Western Antiquity." *Journal of Biblical Literature* 109/1: 3–27.

Alexander, Loveday. 1990. "The Living Voice: Scepticism towards the Written Word in Early Christian and in Graeco-Roman Texts." In *The Bible in Three Dimensions: Essays in Celebration of Forty Years of Biblical Studies in the University of Sheffield*. Journal for the Study of the Old Testament Supplement Series 87. Edited by D. J. A. Clines, S. E. Fowl, and S. E. Porter. Sheffield: Sheffield Academic Press, 221–47.

—. 2006. "What is a Gospel?" In *The Cambridge Companion to the Gospels*. Edited by S. C. Barton. Cambridge: Cambridge University Press, 13–33.

—. 2009. "Memory and Tradition in the Hellenistic Schools." In *Jesus in Memory: Traditions in Oral and Scribal Perspectives*. Edited by W. H. Kelber and S. Byrskog. Waco, TX: Baylor University Press, 113–53.

Allison, Dale C., Jr. 2000. *The Intertextual Jesus: Scripture in Q*. Harrisburg, PA: Trinity Press International.

—. 2010. *Constructing Jesus: Memory, Imagination, and History*. Grand Rapids: Baker Academic.

Assmann, Jan. 1997. *Moses the Egyptian: The Memory of Egypt in Western Monotheism*. Cambridge, MA: Harvard University Press.

Aune, David E. 1998. *Revelation*. 3 volumes. Word Biblical Commentary 52. Nashville: Thomas Nelson.

—. 2006. *Apocalypticism, Prophecy, and Magic in Early Christianity: Collected Essays*. Grand Rapids: Baker Academic.

—. 2009. "Jesus Tradition and the Pauline Letters." In *Jesus in Memory: Traditions in Oral and Scribal Perspectives*. Edited by W. Kelber and S. Byrskog. Waco, TX: Baylor University Press, 63–86.

Badenas, Robert. 1985. *Christ the End of the Law: Romans 10.4 in Pauline Perspective*. Journal for the Study of the New Testament Supplement Series 10. Sheffield: JSOT Press.

Bailey, Kenneth E. 1991. "Informal Controlled Oral Tradition and the Synoptic Gospels." *Asia Journal of Theology* 5/1: 34–54. Reprinted in *Themelios* 20 (1995a): 4–11 (citations come from the 1995 reprint).

—. 1995b. "Middle Eastern Oral Tradition and the Synoptic Gospels." *The Expository Times* 106/12: 363–7.

Bakker, Egbert J. 1997. *Poetry in Speech: Orality and Homeric Discourse.* Myth and Poetics. Ithaca, NY: Cornell University Press.

—. 1999. "How Oral is Oral Composition?" In *Signs of Orality: The Oral Tradition and its Influence in the Greek and Roman Worlds.* Supplements to Mnemosyne 188. Edited by E. A. Mackay. Leiden: Brill, 29–47.

—. 2005. *Pointing at the Past: From Formula to Performance in Homeric Poetics.* Hellenic Studies 12. Cambridge, MA: Harvard University Press.

Barrett, C. K. 1955. *The Gospel according to St. John: An Introduction with Commentary and Notes on the Greek Text.* (2nd edn 1978). Philadelphia: Westminster Press.

Bascom, William R. 1955. "Verbal Art." *Journal of American Folklore* 68: 245–52.

Bauckham, Richard J. 1993. *The Climax of Prophecy: Studies on the Book of Revelation.* Edinburgh: T&T Clark.

—. 1997. "John for Readers of Mark." In *The Gospels for All Christians: Rethinking the Gospel Audiences.* Edited by R. Bauckham. Grand Rapids: Eerdmans, 147–71.

—. 2006. *Jesus and the Eyewitnesses: The Gospels as Eyewitness Testimony.* Grand Rapids: Eerdmans.

Bauman, Richard. 1992a. "Folklore." In *Folklore, Cultural Performances, and Popular Entertainments: A Communications-centered Handbook.* Edited by R. Bauman. New York: Oxford University Press, 29–40.

—. 1992b. "Performance." In *Folklore, Cultural Performances, and Popular Entertainments: A Communications-centered Handbook.* Edited by R. Bauman. New York: Oxford University Press, 41–9.

Beasley-Murray, George R. 1999. *John.* Word Biblical Commentary 36. 2nd edition. Nashville: Thomas Nelson.

Bitzer, Lloyd F. 1968. "The Rhetorical Situation." *Philosophy and Rhetoric* 1/1: 1–14.

Botha, Pieter J. J. 1990. "Mute Manuscripts: Analysing a Neglected Aspect of Ancient Communication." *Theologia Evangelica* 23/3: 35–47.

—. 1991. "Mark's Story as Oral Traditional Literature: Rethinking the Transmission of Some Traditions about Jesus." *Hervormde Teologiese Studies* 47/2: 304–31.

—. 1992. "Letter Writing and Oral Communication in Antiquity: Suggested Implications for the Interpretation of Paul's Letter to the Galatians." *Scriptura* 42: 17–34.

—. 1993a. "Living Voice and Lifeless Letters: Reserve towards Writing in the Graeco-Roman World." *Hervormde Teologiese Studies* 49/4: 742–59.

—. 1993b. "The Verbal Art of the Pauline Letters: Rhetoric, Performance and Presence." In *Rhetoric and the New Testament: Essays from the 1992 Heidelberg Conference.* Journal for the Study of the New Testament Supplement Series 90. Edited by S. E. Porter and T. H. Olbricht. Sheffield: Sheffield Academic Press, 409–28.

—. 2004. "Cognition, Orality-Literacy, and Approaches to First-Century Writings." In *Orality, Literacy, and Colonialism in Antiquity.* Semeia Studies 47. Edited by J. A. Draper. Atlanta: Society of Biblical Literature, 37–63.

—. 2005. "New Testament Texts in the Context of Reading Practices of the Roman Period: The Role of Memory and Performance." *Scriptura* 90: 621–40.

—. 2009a. "Authorship in Historical Perspective and its Bearing on New Testament and Early Christian Texts and Contexts." *Scriptura* 102: 495–510.

—. 2009b. "The Greco-Roman Book: Contextualising Early Christian Documents." *Acta Patristica et Byzantina* 20: 2–27.

Boyarin, Daniel. 2004. *Border Lines: The Partition of Judaeo-Christianity.* Divinations: Rereading Late Ancient Religion. Philadelphia: University of Pennsylvania Press.

Bultmann, Rudolf. 1963. *History of the Synoptic Tradition.* Translated by John Marsh. Oxford: Basil Blackwell.

—. 1971. *The Gospel of John: A Commentary.* Translated by G. R. Beasley-Murray. Philadelphia: Westminster Press.

Burnyeat, M. F. 1997. "Postscript on Silent Reading." *The Classical Quarterly* 47/1: 74–76.

Byrskog, Samuel. 2000. *Story as History, History as Story: The Gospel Tradition in the Context of Ancient Oral Historiography.* Wissenschaftliche Untersuchungen zum Neuen Testament 123. Tübingen: Mohr Siebeck.

Caneday, A. B. 1999. "Mark's Provocative Use of Scripture in Narration: 'He was with the Wild Animals and Angels Ministered to Him.'" *Bulletin for Biblical Research* 9: 19–36.

Carr, David M. 2005. *Writing on the Tablet of the Heart: Origins of Scripture and Literature.* Oxford: Oxford University Press.

Carson, D. A., Douglas J. Moo, and Leon Morris. 1992. *An Introduction to the New Testament.* Grand Rapids: Zondervan. Second edition: 2005.

Cartlidge, David R. 1990. "Combien d'unités avez-vous de trois à quatre? What Do We Mean by Intertextuality in Early Church

Studies?" In *SBL Seminar Papers* 29. Edited by D. J. Lull. Atlanta:
Scholars Press, 400–11.

Casey, Maurice. 2010. *Jesus of Nazareth: An Independent Historian's
Account of his Life and Teaching.* London: T&T Clark International.

Charles, Robert Henry. 1920. *A Critical and Exegetical Commentary
on the Revelation of St John.* 2 volumes. International Critical
Commentary. New York: Charles Scribner's Sons.

Choat, Malcolm and Rachel Yuen-Collingridge. 2009. "A Church with
No Books and a Reader Who Cannot Write: The Strange Case of
P.Oxy. 33.2673." *Bulletin of the American Society of Papyrologists*
46: 109–38.

Craffert, Pieter F. and Pieter J. J. Botha. 2005. "Why Jesus Could
Walk on the Sea but He Could Not Read and Write: Reflections
on Historicity and Interpretation in Historical Jesus Research."
Neotestamenica 39/1: 5–35.

Crossley, James G. 2004. *The Date of Mark's Gospel: Insight from
the Law in Earliest Christianity.* Journal for the Study of the New
Testament Supplement Series 266. London: T&T Clark International.

—. 2010. *The New Testament and Jewish Law.* A Guide for the
Perplexed. London: T&T Clark International.

Culpepper, Alan R. 1983. *Anatomy of the Fourth Gospel: A Study in
Literary Design.* Philadelphia: Fortress Press.

Davis, Casey W. 1999. *Oral Biblical Criticism: The Influence of the
Principles of Orality on the Literary Structure of Paul's Epistle to the
Philippians.* Journal for the Study of the New Testament Supplement
Series 172. Sheffield: Sheffield Academic Press.

—. 2008. "Hebrews 6:4–6 from an Oral Critical Perspective." *Journal
of the Evangelical Theological Society* 51/4: 753–67.

Dewey, Arthur J. 1995. "A Re-Hearing of Romans 10:1–15." In *Orality
and Textuality in Early Christian Literature.* Semeia 65. Edited by
J. Dewey. Atlanta: Society of Biblical Literature, 109–27.

Dewey, Joanna. 1973. "The Literary Structure of the Controversy Stories
in Mark 2:1–3:6." *Journal of Biblical Literature* 92/3: 394–401.

—. 1980. *Markan Public Debate: Literary Technique, Concentric
Structure and Theology in Mark 2:1–3:6.* Society of Biblical
Literature Dissertation Series 48. Chico, CA: Scholars Press.

—. 1989. "Oral Methods of Structuring Narrative in Mark."
Interpretation 43/1: 32–44.

—. 1991. "Mark as Interwoven Tapestry: Forecasts and Echoes for a
Listening Audience." *Catholic Biblical Quarterly* 53/2: 221–36.

—. 1992. "Mark as Aural Narrative: Structures as Clues to
Understanding." *Sewanee Theological Review* 36/1: 45–56.

—. 1995. "Textuality in an Oral Culture: A Survey of the Pauline
Traditions." In *Orality and Textuality in Early Christian Literature.*

Semeia 65. Edited by J. Dewey. Atlanta: Society of Biblical
Literature, 37–65.
—. 2008. "The Gospel of Mark as Oral Hermeneutic." In *Jesus, the
Voice, and the Text: Beyond* The Oral and the Written Gospel.
Edited by T. Thatcher. Waco, TX: Baylor University Press, 71–87.
Dewey, Joanna, ed. 1995. *Orality and Textuality in Early Christian
Literature.* Semeia 65. Atlanta: Scholars Press.
Dibelius, Martin. 1935. *From Tradition to Gospel.* Translated by
Bertram Lee Woolf. New York: Charles Scribner's Sons.
Dunn, James D. G. 1988. *Romans.* 2 volumes. Word Biblical
Commentary 38. Nashville: Thomas Nelson.
—. 2003a. "Altering the default setting: re-envisaging the early
transmission of the Jesus tradition." *New Testament Studies* 49/2:
139–75. Reprinted in Dunn 2005: 79–125 (citations come from the
2005 reprint).
—. 2003b. *Jesus Remembered.* Christianity in the Making 1. Grand
Rapids and Cambridge: Eerdmans.
—. 2005. *A New Perspective on Jesus: What the Quest for the
Historical Jesus Missed.* London: SPCK.
—. 2009. "Kenneth Bailey's Theory of Oral Tradition: Critiquing
Theodore Weeden's Critique." *Journal for the Study of the Historical
Jesus* 7/1: 44–62.
Edwards, James R. 2002. *The Gospel According to Mark.* The Pillar
New Testament Commentary. Grand Rapids: Eerdmans.
Ehrman, Bart D. 1993. *The Orthodox Corruption of Scripture: The
Effect of Early Christological Controversies on the Text of the New
Testament.* Oxford: Oxford University Press.
—. 2005. *Misquoting Jesus: The Story behind Who Changed the Bible
and Why.* San Francisco: HarperCollins.
Elman, Yaakov. 1999. "Orality and the Redaction of the Babylonian
Talmud." *Oral Tradition* 14/1: 52–99.
Evans, Craig A. 2004. "Sorting out the Synoptic Problem: Why an Old
Approach is Still Best." In *Reading the Gospels Today.* Edited by
S. Porter. Grand Rapids: Eerdmans, 1–26.
Fekkes, Jan. 1994. *Isaiah and Prophetic Traditions in the Book of
Revelation: Visionary Antecedents and their Development.* Journal
for the Study of the New Testament Supplement Series 93. Sheffield:
JSOT Press.
Finnegan, Ruth. 1990. "What is Orality—if Anything?" *Byzantine and
Modern Greek Studies* 14: 130–49.
Foley, John Miles. 1988. *The Theory of Oral Composition: History and
Methodology.* Bloomington, IN: Indiana University Press.
—. 1991. *Immanent Art: From Structure to meaning in Traditional
Oral Epic.* Bloomington, IN: Indiana University Press.

—. 1995a. *The Singer of Tales in Performance*. Voices in Performance
  and Text. Bloomington, IN: Indiana University Press.
—. 1995b. "Words in Tradition, Words in Text: A Response." In *Orality
  and Textuality in Early Christian Literature*. Semeia 65. Edited by
  J. Dewey. Atlanta: Society of Biblical Literature, 169–80.
—. 1999. "What's in a Sign?" In *Signs of Orality: The Oral Tradition
  and its Influence in the Greek and Roman Worlds*. Supplements to
  Mnemosyne 188. Edited by E. Anne Mackay. Leiden: Brill, 1–27.
—. 2006. "The Riddle of Q: Oral Ancestor, Textual Precedent, or
  Ideological Creation?" In *Oral Performance, Popular Tradition, and
  Hidden Transcript in Q*. Semeia. Edited by R. A. Horsley. Atlanta:
  Society of Biblical Literature, 123–40.
France, Richard T. 2002. *The Gospel of Mark: A Commentary on
  the Greek Text*. New International Greek Testament Commentary.
  Grand Rapids: Eerdmans.
Fuchs, Ernst. 1964. "The Quest of the Historical Jesus." In *Studies
  of the Historical Jesus*. Translated by A. Scobie. Studies in Biblical
  Theology 42. London: SCM, 1964, 11–31.
Fusi, Alessandra. 2003. "The Oral/Literate Model: A Valid Approach
  for New Testament Studies?" PhD Thesis. Sheffield: The University of
  Sheffield.
Gamble, Harry Y. 1995. *Books and Readers in the Early Church: A
  History of Early Christian Texts*. New Haven, CT: Yale University
  Press.
Gavrilov, A. K. 1997. "Techniques of Reading in Classical Antiquity."
  The Classical Quarterly 47/1: 56–73.
Gerhardsson, Birger. 1961. *Memory and Manuscript: Oral Tradition
  and Written Transmission in Rabbinic Judaism and Early
  Christianity*. Acta Seminarii Neotestamentici Upsaliensis 22.
  Translated by E. J. Sharpe. Lund: C. W. K. Gleerup. Republished
  with *Tradition and Transmission* by Eerdmans (1998).
—. 1964. *Tradition and Transmission in Early Christianity*.
  Coniectanea Neotestamentica 20. Translated by E. J. Sharpe. Lund:
  C. W. K. Gleerup. Republished with *Memory and Manuscript* by
  Eerdmans (1998).
—. 1991. "Illuminating the Kingdom: Narrative Meshalim in the
  Synoptic Gospels." *Jesus and the Oral Gospel Tradition*. Journal
  for the Study of the New Testament Supplement Series 64. Edited by
  H. Wansbrough. Sheffield: Sheffield Academic Press, 266–309.
—. 2001. *The Reliability of the Gospel Tradition*. With a foreword by
  D. A. Hagner. Peabody, MA: Hendrickson.
—. 2005. "The Secret of the Transmission of the Unwritten Jesus
  Tradition." *New Testament Studies* 51: 1–18.

Gilliard, Frank D. 1993. "More Silent Reading in Antiquity: *Non Omne Verbum Sonat.*" *Journal of Biblical Literature* 112/4: 689–94.

Gombis, Timothy G. 2010. *Paul. A Guide for the Perplexed.* London: T&T Clark International.

Goodacre, Mark. 2002. *The Case against Q: Studies in Markan Priority and the Synoptic Problem.* Harrisburg, PA: Trinity Press International.

—. 2012. Thomas *and the Gospels: The Case for* Thomas's *Familiarity with the Synoptics.* Grand Rapids: Eerdmans.

Goody, Jack and Ian Watt. 1968. "The Consequences of Literacy." Reprinted in *Perspectives on Literacy* [1988]. Edited by E. R. Kintgen, B. M. Kroll, and M. Rose. Carbondale, IL: Southern Illinois University Press, 3–27.

Graham, William A. 1987. *Beyond the Written Word: Oral Aspects of Scripture in the History of Religion.* Cambridge: Cambridge University Press.

Green, Joel B., Scot McKnight, and I. Howard Marshall, eds. 1992. *Dictionary of Jesus and the Gospels.* Downers Grove, IL: InterVarsity Press.

Harris, William V. 1989. *Ancient Literacy.* Cambridge: Harvard University Press.

Harvey, John D. 1998. *Listening to the Text: Oral Patterning in Paul's Letters.* Evangelical Theological Society Studies Series 1. Grand Rapids: Baker.

Havelock, Eric A. 1963. *Preface to Plato.* Cambridge: Belknap of Harvard University.

—. 1984. "Oral Composition in the *Oedipus Tyrannus* of Sophocles." *New Literary History* 16/1: 175–97.

Hays, Richard B. 1989. *Echoes of Scripture in the Letters of Paul.* New Haven, CT: Yale University Press.

Hearon, Holly E. 2008. "Storytelling in Oral and Written Media Contexts of the Ancient Mediterranean World." In *Jesus, the Voice, and the Text: Beyond* The Oral and the Written Gospel. Edited by T. Thatcher. Waco, TX: Baylor University Press, 89–110.

Heil, John Paul. 2006. "Jesus with the Wild Animals in Mark 1:13." *Catholic Biblical Quarterly* 68/1: 63–78.

Hezser, Catherine. 2001. *Jewish Literacy in Roman Palestine.* Texts and Studies in Ancient Judaism 81. Tübingen: Mohr Siebeck.

Hoffmann, Joseph R. 1987. *Celsus: On the True Doctrine: A Discourse against the Christians.* New York: Oxford University Press.

Holmes, Michael W. 2007. *The Apostolic Fathers: Greek Texts and English Translations.* 3rd edn. Grand Rapids: Baker Academic.

Holtz, Traugott. 1991. "Paul and the Oral Gospel Tradition." In *Jesus and the Oral Gospel Tradition.* Journal for the Study of the

New Testament: Supplement Series 64. Edited by H. Wansbrough. Sheffield: Sheffield Academic Press, 380–93.

Hooker, Morna D. 1970. "Christology and Methodology." *New Testament Studies* 17: 480–7.

—. 1972. "On Using the Wrong Tool." *Theology* 75: 570–81.

Horsley, Richard A. 1994. "Innovation in Search of Reorientation: New Testament Studies Rediscovering its Subject Matter." *Journal of the American Academy of Religion* 62/4: 1127–66.

—. 2001. *Hearing the Whole Story: The Politics of Plot in Mark's Gospel.* Louisville, KY: Westminster John Knox Press.

—. 2010. "Oral and Written Aspects of the Emergence of the Gospel of Mark as Scripture." *Oral Tradition* 25/1: 93–114.

Horsley, Richard A., with Jonathan A. Draper. 1999. *Whoever Hears You Hears Me: Prophets, Performance, and Tradition in Q.* Harrisburg, PA: Trinity Press International.

Horsley, Richard A., Jonathan A. Draper, and John Miles Foley, eds. 2006. *Performing the Gospel: Orality, Memory, and Mark. Essays Dedicated to Werner Kelber.* Minneapolis: Fortress Press.

Hurtado, Larry W. 1985. "Revelation 4–5 in the Light of Jewish Apocalyptic Analogies." *Journal for the Study of the New Testament* 25: 105–24.

—. 1989. *Mark.* New International Biblical Commentary. Peabody, MA: Hendrickson.

—. 1997. "Greco-Roman Textuality and the Gospel of Mark: A Critical Assessment of Werner Kelber's *The Oral and the Written Gospel.*" *Bulletin for Biblical Research* 7: 91–106.

Ito, Akio. 2006. "The Written Torah and the Oral Gospel: Romans 10:5–13 in the Dynamic Tension between Orality and Literacy." *Novum Testamentum* 48/3: 234–60.

Iverson, Kelly R. 2009. "Orality and the Gospels: A Survey of Recent Research." *Currents in Biblical Research* 8/1: 71–106.

Jewett, Robert. 2007. *Romans.* Hermeneia. Minneapolis: Fortress Press.

Johnson, William A. 2000. "Toward a Sociology of Reading in Classical Antiquity." *The American Journal of Philology* 121/4: 593–627.

—. 2010. *Readers and Reading Culture in the High Roman Empire: A Study of Elite Communities.* Classical Culture and Society. Oxford: Oxford University Press.

Keightley, Georgia Masters. 2005. "Christian Collective Memory and Paul's Knowledge of Jesus." In *Memory, Tradition, and Text: Uses of the Past in Early Christianity.* Semeia Studies 52. Edited by A. Kirk and T. Thatcher. Atlanta: Society of Biblical Literature, 129–50.

Keith, Chris. 2009. *The Pericope Adulterae, the Gospel of John, and the Literacy of Jesus.* New Testament Tools, Studies and Documents 38. Leiden: Brill.

—. 2010. "The Claim of John 7.15 and the Memory of Jesus' Literacy." *New Testament Studies* 56/1: 44–63.

—. 2011a. *Jesus' Literacy: Scribal Culture and the Teacher from Galilee.* Library of Historical Jesus Studies 8. Library of New Testament Studies 413. London: T&T Clark International.

—. 2011b. "Memory and Authenticity: Jesus Tradition and What Really Happened." *Zeitschrift für die neutestamentliche Wissenschaft und die Kunder der älteren Kirche* 102: 155–77.

—. 2012. "The Indebtedness of the Criteria Approach to Form Criticism and Recent Attempts to Rehabilitate the Search for an Authentic Jesus." In *Jesus, Criteria, and the Demise of Authenticity.* Edited by C. Keith and A. Le Donne. London: T&T Clark International, 25–48.

—. forthcoming. "Prolegomena on the Textualization of Mark's Gospel: Manuscript Culture, the Extended Situation, and the Emergence of the Written Gospel." In *Keys and Frames: Memory and Identity in Ancient Judaism and Early Christianity.* Semeia Studies. Edited by T. Thatcher. Atlanta: Society of Biblical Literature.

Keith, Chris and Anthony Le Donne, eds. 2012. *Jesus, Criteria, and the Demise of Authenticity.* London: T&T Clark International.

Kelber, Werner H. 1983. *The Oral and the Written Gospel: The Hermeneutics of Speaking and Writing in the Synoptic Tradition, Mark, Paul, and Q.* Philadelphia: Fortress Press. Reissued in 1997 by Indiana University Press.

—. 1995. "Jesus and Tradition: Words in Time, Words in Space." In *Orality and Textuality in Early Christian Literature.* Semeia 65. Edited by J. Dewey. Atlanta: Society of Biblical Literature, 139–67.

—. 1997. "Introduction." *The Oral and the Written Gospel: The Hermeneutics of Speaking and Writing in the Synoptic Tradition, Mark, Paul, and Q.* Voices in Performance and Text. Bloomington, IN: Indiana University Press, xix–xxxi.

—. 2009. "Conclusion: The Work of Birger Gerhardsson in Perspective." In *Jesus in Memory: Traditions in Oral and Scribal Perspectives.* Edited by W. Kelber and S. Byrskog. Waco, TX: Baylor University Press, 173–206.

—. 2010. "The History of the Closure of Biblical Texts." In *The Interface of Orality and Writing: Speaking, Seeing, Writing in the Shaping of New Genres.* Wissenschaftliche Untersuchungen zum Neuen Testament 260. Edited by A. Weissenrieder and R. Coote. Tübingen: Mohr Siebeck, 2010, 71–99.

Kelber, Werner H. and Samuel Byrskog, eds. 2009. *Jesus in Memory: Traditions in Oral and Scribal Perspectives.* Waco, TX: Baylor University Press.

Kelber, Werner H. and Tom Thatcher. 2008. "'It's Not Easy to Take a Fresh Approach': Reflections on *The Oral and the Written Gospel* (an Interview with Werner Kelber)." In *Jesus, the Voice, and the Text: Beyond* The Oral and the Written Gospel. Edited by T. Thatcher. Waco, TX: Baylor University Press, 27–43.

Kirk, Alan. 2008. "Manuscript Tradition as a *Tertium Quid*: Orality and Memory in Scribal Practices." In *Jesus, the Voice, and the Text: Beyond* The Oral and the Written Gospel. Edited by T. Thatcher. Waco, TX: Baylor University Press, 215–34.

Kirk, Alan and Tom Thatcher, eds. 2005. *Memory, Tradition, and Text: Uses of the Past in Early Christianity*. Semeia Studies 52. Atlanta: Society of Biblical Literature.

Koester, Craig R. 2001. *Revelation and the End of All Things*. Grand Rapids: Eerdmans.

Köstenberger, Andreas J. 2004. *John*. Baker Exegetical Commentary on the New Testament. Grand Rapids: Baker Academic.

Le Donne, Anthony and Tom Thatcher, eds. 2011. *The Fourth Gospel in First-Century Media Culture*. European Studies on Christian Origins. Library of New Testament Studies 426. London: T&T Clark International.

Lincoln, Andrew T. 2005. *The Gospel according to Saint John*. Black's New Testament Commentaries. London: Continuum.

Linton, Gregory L. 1993. *Intertextuality in the Revelation of John*. PhD Thesis. Durham, NC: Duke University.

Lohr, Charles H. 1961. "Oral Techniques in the Gospel of Matthew." *Catholic Biblical Quarterly* 23/4: 403–35.

Lord, Albert B. 1960. *The Singer of Tales*. Harvard Studies in Comparative Literature 24. Cambridge: Harvard University Press.

—. 1978. "The Gospels as Oral Traditional Literature." In *Relationships among the Gospels: An Interdisciplinary Dialogue*. Edited by W. O. Walker. San Antonio, TX: Trinity University Press, 33–91.

Marcus, Joel. 1992. *The Way of the Lord: Christological Exegesis of the Old Testament in the Gospel of Mark*. Louisville, KY: Westminster John Knox.

Mauser, Ulrich W. 1963. *Christ in the Wilderness: The Wilderness Theme in the Second Gospel and Its Basis in the Biblical Tradition*. Studies in Biblical Theology 39. Naperville, IL: Allenson.

Maxey, James A. 2009. *From Orality to Orality: A New Paradigm for Contextual Translation of the Bible*. Biblical Performance Criticism 2. Eugene, OR: Cascade Books.

Metzger, Bruce M. and Bart D. Ehrman. 2005. *The Text of the New Testament: Its Transmission, Corruption, and Restoration*. 4th edition. Oxford: Oxford University Press.

Michaels, Ramsey J. 2010. *The Gospel of John*. New International Commentary on the New Testament. Grand Rapids: Eerdmans.

Morris, Leon. 1995. *The Gospel according to John*. New International Commentary on the New Testament. Grand Rapids: Eerdmans.

Mournet, Terence. 2005. *Oral Tradition and Literary Dependency: Variability and Stability in the Synoptic Tradition and Q*. Wissenschaftliche Untersuchungen zum Neuen Testament 2/195. Tübingen: Mohr Siebeck.

Moyise, Steve. 1995. *The Old Testament in the Book of Revelation*. Journal for the Study of the New Testament Supplement Series 115. Sheffield: Sheffield Academic Press.

North, Wendy E. Sproston. 2003. "John for Readers of Mark? A Response to Richard Bauckham's Proposal." *Journal for the Study of the New Testament* 25/4: 449–68.

O'Grady, John F. 2007. "The Prologue and Chapter 17 of the Gospel of John." In *What We Have Heard from the Beginning: The Past, Present, and Future of Johannine Studies*. Edited by T. Thatcher. Waco, TX: Baylor University Press, 215–28.

Ong, Walter. 1971. *Rhetoric, Romance, and Technology*. Ithaca, NY: Cornell University Press.

—. 1978. "Technology Outside Us and Inside Us." *Communio* 5/2: 100–21.

—. 1982. *Orality and Literacy: The Technologizing of the Word*. London: Methuen.

Osborne, Grant R. 2002. *Revelation*. Baker Exegetical Commentary on the New Testament. Grand Rapids: Baker Academic.

Parker, David C. 1997. *The Living Text of the Gospels*. Cambridge: Cambridge University Press.

Resseguie, James L. 2009. *The Revelation of John: A Narrative Commentary*. Grand Rapids: Baker Academic.

Rhoads, David. 2006a. "Performance Criticism: An Emerging Methodology in Second Testament Studies—.Part I." *Biblical Theology Bulletin* 36: 1–16.

—. 2006b. "Performance Criticism: An Emerging Methodology in Second Testament Studies—.Part II." *Biblical Theology Bulletin* 36: 164–84.

Rodríguez, Rafael. 2009. "Reading and Hearing in Ancient Contexts." *Journal for the Study of the New Testament* 32/2: 151–78.

—. 2010. *Structuring Early Christian Memory: Jesus in Tradition, Performance and Text*. European Studies on Christian Origins. Library of New Testament Studies 407. London: T&T Clark International.

Sanders, E. P. 1969. *The Tendencies of the Synoptic Tradition*. Society for New Testament Studies Monograph Series 9. Cambridge: Cambridge University Press.

Schmidt, Karl. 1919. *Der Rahmen der Geschichte Jesu*. Berlin:
Trowitzsch & Sohn.

Schnackenburg, Rudolf. 1968. *The Gospel according to St John*. 3
volumes. Herder's Theological Commentary on the New Testament.
Translated by K. Smyth. New York: Herder and Herder.

Shiner, Whitney. 2003. *Proclaiming the Gospel: First-Century
Performance of Mark*. Harrisburg, PA: Trinity Press International.

—. 2009. "Oral Performance in the New Testament World." In *The
Bible in Ancient and Modern Media: Story and Performance*. Biblical
Performance Criticism 1. Edited by H. E. Hearon and P. Ruge-Jones.
Eugene, OR: Cascade Books, 49–63.

Silberman, Lou, ed. 1987. *Orality, Aurality, and Biblical Narrative*.
Semeia 39. Decatur, GA: Scholars Press.

Smith, Morton. 1963. "A Comparison of Early Christian and Early
Rabbinic Tradition." *Journal of Biblical Literature* 82/2: 169–76.

Stefanović, Ranko. 1996. *The Backgrounds and Meaning of the Sealed
Book of Revelation 5*. Andrews University Seminary Doctoral
Dissertation Series 22. Berrien Springs, MI: Andrews University
Press.

Stein, Robert H. 2008. *Mark*. Baker Exegetical Commentary on the
New Testament. Grand Rapids: Baker Academic.

Stock, Brian. 1983. *The Implications of Literacy: Written Language
and Models of Interpretation in the Eleventh and Twelfth Centuries*.
Princeton: Princeton University Press.

Strauss, Mark L. 2007. *Four Portraits, One Jesus: An Introduction to
Jesus and the Gospels*. Grand Rapids: Zondervan.

Talbert, Charles H. 1974. *Literary Patterns, Theological Themes and
the Genre of Luke-Acts*. Society of Biblical Literature Monograph
Series 20. Missoula, MT: Scholars Press.

Taylor, Vincent. 1933. *The Formation of the Gospel Tradition*. London:
Macmillan and Co.

Thatcher, Tom. 2011. "The Riddle of the Baptist and the Genesis of
the Prologue: John 1.1–18 in Oral/Aural Media Culture." In *The
Fourth Gospel in First-Century Media Culture*. European Studies
on Christian Origins. Library of New Testament Studies 426. Edited
by A. Le Donne and T. Thatcher. London: T&T Clark International,
29–48.

Thatcher, Tom, ed. 2008. *Jesus, the Voice, and the Text: Beyond* The
Oral and the Written Gospel. Waco, TX: Baylor University Press.

Thomas, Rosalind. 1992. *Literacy and Orality in Ancient Greece*. Key
Themes in Ancient History. Cambridge: Cambridge University Press.

Tödt, Heinz Eduard. 1965. *The Son of Man in the Synoptic Tradition*.
Translated by D. M. Barton. Philadelphia: Westminster Press.

von Wahlde, Urban C. 2010. *The Gospel and Letters of John*. 3 volumes. Eerdmans Critical Commentary. Grand Rapids: Eerdmans.

Wallace, Daniel B. 1996. *Greek Grammar beyond the Basics: An Exegetical Syntax of the New Testament*. Grand Rapids: Zondervan.

Ward, Richard F. 1995. "Pauline Voice and Presence as Strategic Communication." In *Orality and Textuality in Early Christian Literature*. Semeia 65. Edited by J. Dewey. Atlanta: Society of Biblical Literature, 95–107.

Weeden, Theodore J., Sr. 1979. "Metaphysical Implications of Kelber's Approach to Orality and Textuality: A Response to Werner Kelber's, 'Mark and the Oral Tradition.'" In *SBL Seminar Papers, 1979*. 2 vols. Edited by P. J. Achtemeier. Society of Biblical Literature Seminar Papers 17. Missoula, MT: Scholars Press, 2:153–66.

—. 2009. "Kenneth Bailey's Theory of Oral Tradition: A Theory Contested by its Evidence." *Journal for the Study of the Historical Jesus* 7/1: 3–43.

Weissenrieder, Annette and Robert B. Coote, eds. 2010. *The Interface of Orality and Writing: Speaking, Seeing, Writing in the Shaping of New Genres*. Wissenschaftliche Untersuchungen Zum Neuen Testament 260. Tübingen: Mohr Siebeck.

Witherington, Ben, III, with Darlene Hyatt. 2004. *Paul's Letter to the Romans: A Socio-Rhetorical Commentary*. Grand Rapids: Eerdmans.

Wright, N. T. 1996. *Jesus and the Victory of God*. Christian Origians and the Question of God 2. Minneapolis: Fortress Press.

—. 2002. "The Letter to the Romans: Introduction, Commentary, and Reflections." In *The New Interpreter's Bible: A Commentary in Twelve Volumes*. Volume 10. Edited by Leander E. Keck. Nashville: Abingdon Press, 393–770.

Yarbro Collins, Adela. 2007. *Mark: A Commentary*. Hermeneia. Minneapolis: Fortress Press.

Young, Stephen E. 2011. *Jesus Tradition in the Apostolic Fathers*. Wissenschaftliche Untersuchungen zum Neuen Testament 2/311. Tübingen: Mohr Siebeck.

TEXT INDEX

Other Ancient Writings

AUTHOR INDEX

SUBJECT INDEX